The Lean Coach

Developing the Habits of Continuous Improvement

By

Lawrence M. Miller

Email: LMMiller@lmmiller.com

Published by

Miller Management Press, LLC

Books are available at special quantity discounts to use as premiums and sales promotions, or for use in corporate training programs. Please email the author for arrangements.

For more information, please visit www.ManagementMeditations.com and www.lmmiller.com/online-learning/ for information on related online courses and materials.

ISBN: 978-0-9893232-9-1

Filed with the U.S. Copyright Office (1-3784102701)

CONTENTS

Other Books by Lawrence M. Miller

Team Kata - The Foundation of Lean Culture

Getting to Lean - Transformational Change Management

Lean Culture - The Leader's Guide

HealthCare Lean - The Team Guide to Continuous Improvement.

Barbarians to Bureaucrats: Corporate Life Cycle Strategies

Spiritual Enterprise: Building Your Business in the Spirit of Service

American Spirit: Visions of a New Corporate Culture

From Management to Leadership

Team Management: Creating Systems and Skills for a Team Based Organization

Change Management: Creating the Dynamic Organization through Whole System Architecture

Behavior Management: The New Science of Managing People at Work

Online Courses

Team Leadership - The Kata of Lean Culture

Coaching Teams and Team Leaders

Strategy Execution - The Agile/Lean Way

Motivation: The Science of Motivating Yourself and Others

Team Leadership: Facilitating High Performing Teams

Leadership and Life Cycles

Creating Wealth in Your Life and Business

Problem-Solving Made Easy

Website: www.ManagementMeditations.com

Email: LMMiller@lmmiller.com

ACKNOWLEDGEMENT

I owe everything to my clients. Without them I would know nothing and my advice would be worthless. I have been incredibly blessed to have worked with some of the finest companies in the world and some truly excellent leaders. They have always challenged me to think beyond my current framework and develop new approaches to new challenges.

In the past few years I have been fortunate to work with VON Canada. Sharon Goodwin has been the true lean leader and change champion who has been a great partner. Louisa Yue Chan has been the leader of their Lean Center of Excellence and has contributed to the development of Lean Coaches.

My relationship with editors has always been a tortured one. "Why must there be a comma there! It makes no sense." I've learned to just do it. Nadia Saad has been a diligent and patient editor and whatever isn't right now... well, you should have seen it before editing!

INTRODUCTION

To change the culture of an organization you must change the habit patterns of both leaders and followers – the patterns of behavior, thought and emotion. Culture is the sum of our beliefs and habits. Individuals rarely change their habits without the assistance of a coach, and companies rarely provide the needed coaching. This is the problem. What follows is a solution.

Most organizations are adopting lean culture. Many are struggling because of their inability to instill a sustainable change in the habits of continuous improvement, problem-solving, and effective team leadership. The cost of external coaching is too great, and most companies do not have sufficient internal full-time coaches. The only solution is for operating managers to develop coaching skills, and provide coaching to both their own team and to other peer managers and teams. This is the *Lean Coach*. This book and companion online course are intended to provide the needed coaching process and skills to instill the habits of lean culture.[1]

There are two bodies of knowledge upon which the methods in this book are based. The first is *lean management* (derived from the Toyota Production System). The second is *behavior analysis* or *behavioral psychology* which focuses on behavior, not personality or internal mental states. It can be summarized by the phrase *"It is easier to act your way into a new way of feeling, than feel your way into a new way of acting."* Both of these approaches employ the scientific method, focusing on data and experimentation. They are both practical and can be used in the workplace without advanced training.

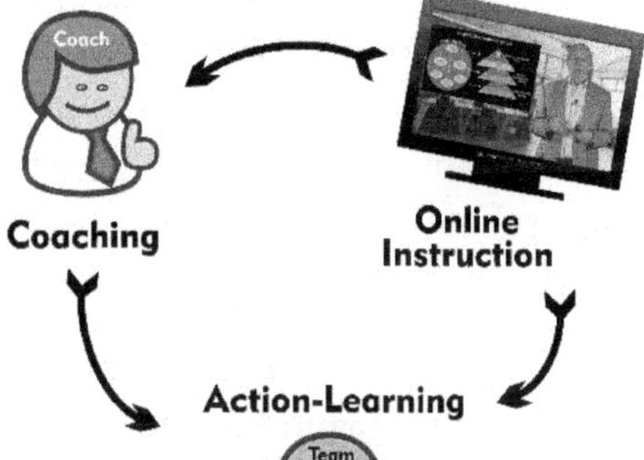

[1] See the author's online learning courses for coaches, teams and team leaders at www.lmmiller.com/online-learning. This book is a companion to the author's *Team Kata* book and course.

Leaders and their organizations are discovering that the most effective and efficient means of training is a *blended learning* model in which students a) acquire small bits of knowledge, often through online learning; b) practice new behavior; c) receive feedback and encouragement from a coach; and d) build skills by repeated practice. Sustainable learning occurs from taking action and receiving feedback in the work setting.

This author has been providing coaching to internal change agents, senior managers, teams, and even inmates in prison, for the past forty years. The model of coaching presented here is well proven, tested, and can easily be adopted by any organization.

The internal capability to change behavior through coaching is essential to successful lean implementation. Without this internal capability it is very difficult to sustain changes over a long period of time. We know from the study of lean organizations that to become an excellent organization providing truly superior service to customers, continuous improvement is a requirement, not an option. Continuous improvement is not a program that can be completed within six months or a year. It is a way of life. You can only achieve this if you develop a cadre of lean coaches who become change agents and coach their peers.

This book is not a course on the basics of lean management – the problem-solving, process improvement or team leadership skills. Those skills are provided in my *Team Kata* book and *Team Leadership* online course. But reading a book, attending a workshop, or viewing an online course will not by itself produce a sustained change in behavior. This will only be achieved by an on-going process of training, coaching and feedback. My intention is to provide all the material needed for organizations to adopt this process internally.

The role of the *sensei* has been an essential element of Toyota culture. A *sensei* is a coach and mentor within the organization - someone who can guide, observe, and give feedback and encouragement. It is worth noting that in every sport, whether the emphasis is on team or individual performance, there is always a coach. And coaches are not reserved for novices or poor performers. The best professional quarterbacks, tennis stars, professional golfers and opera singers all have personal coaches, even when they are at the top of their profession.

In a May 2004 Harvard Business Review article (*Learning to Lead at Toyota*) Steven J. Spear does an excellent job describing how a new manager is hired and trained at Toyota.[2] He is assigned a coach who introduces him to the organization and guides him through structured observations and exercises. He is asked to find improvements, many each day, just from observing. Then he is asked to work on the line with an assembly team. He is asked to find improvements and work with the team implementing them. He is then taken to Japan to again work with a frontline team and implement improvements, in the very plant where the Toyota Production System began. At each step the sensei is encouraging him, guiding, and debriefing him on the lessons he is learning. It is an intensely personal sequence of direct training and coaching. But the sensei does little instructing in the traditional sense. Rather, he is creating experiences, asking questions, and encouraging reflection.

Now consider how you develop leaders and teams in your own organization. Do they have a coach? Do they follow a structured learning process? Do they receive guidance, encouragement and feedback from a coach and their manager? Let me suggest that this is a necessity at every level of the organization.

If you have been a manager you may find the coaching role difficult. As a coach you give up power and adopt the role of guiding and encouraging. It is not easy to be someone whose role is to coach rather than manage. Here are some quick suggestions:

What is the Role of a *Lean Coach*?

- To assist others to develop the habits of eliminating waste and to pursue continuous improvement.
- To learn and practice the skills of leading teams in the process of lean and agile continuous improvement and problem-solving.
- To guide and assist peer managers and teams in their development.
- To provide structured feedback to managers and team leaders to encourage and guide their learning.

---

[2] Spear, Steven J. Harvard Business Review. *Learning to Lead at Toyota*. May, 2004.

- To challenge managers and teams to analyse current performance and set targets for improved performance.

YOU WILL SUCCEED IF....

- You are clear who you are working for - your client and the sponsoring manager.
- You give a priority to meeting the needs of your client and your organization, not to implementing *your* program, *your* plan, or *your* methods. It's about them, not you!
- You have the courage and ability to provide honest feedback in a caring manner.
- You are continually willing to adapt to changing circumstances, and you are willing to learn from others and from your own results.
- You model the behavior of teamwork, problem-solving, and know the data.
- You focus on measurable performance and pinpointed behavior rather than on attitudes.
- You bring joy to your work and encourage others.

PART ONE

THE PRINCIPLES AND PROCESS OF LEAN COACHING

Chapter 1

Models of Coaching & The Toyota Way

Coaching is becoming widespread in our organizations with many people claiming to be coaches, but with very different interests and skills. To those implementing lean management, it is important to recognize that every manager at Toyota has a coach or mentor. In most cases these are other managers. This mentor-mentee relationship is central to lean culture and the improvement process.

Every coach assists others in their learning or change processes, but the roles and priorities may differ dramatically. The priorities of the coach and client should be in alignment and they should be clear.

Some coaches have received very quick and simple training following the Toyota Kata method, and some have received years of training in university courses, and may have received certification by the International Coaching Federation.

Let's distinguish between the different types of coaching and the intent of *Lean Coaching* as I am presenting it in this book:

Life Coaching:

This is a common coaching relationship focused on the personal objectives of an individual client. This may include helping the individual lose weight, finally getting that book written, or gaining the assertiveness to ask for that raise at work. This type of coaching calls upon the coach to put aside her own agenda and focus on the agenda of the client. A life coach does not deal with psychological problems but helps the client to achieve her goals. It is not psychotherapy aimed at resolving psychological problems. The life coach is trained to resist the temptation to give advice, but guides the client through identifying and selecting from possible courses of action.

Life coaching is also not linked to the goals of any organization. In this respect it differs significantly from lean coaching which is linked to the goals of the organization.

Executive Coaching:

An executive coach may have his or her own executive experience and works with the client executive to both improve his or her leadership style, serving as a sounding board, and as a source of feedback regarding strategic decisions faced by the executive. An executive coach should have sufficient business or executive experience to provide advice on business decisions. Executive coaching is not focused on the executive's behavior or needs outside of work. The focus is on the executive's effectiveness and on his impact on the organization's performance.

One assumption about executive coaching is that the higher you rise in an organization, and therefore the more power you have, the less likely it is that others in the organization will give you direct and frank feedback. In executive coaching, the confidential relationship between the executive and the client is very important.

Business Coaching or Management Consulting:

A business coach or consultant is focused on improving the performance of an organization. He may focus on the whole-system of the organization, or on specific sub-systems, such as a work process, information systems, finance or marketing. He may have a specialty such as lean manufacturing, organization culture or finance. When the focus is on the overall performance of an organization, the coach/consultant must have broad business knowledge and an understanding of how the systems of an organization interact with one another. For example, if the consultant is recommending a change in the organization's structure, he must understand that the information systems will need to be re-aligned to support that new structure. Similarly, if he is working to improve the culture of the organization, he must understand how the senior team and executive's behavior impact that culture, and be willing to address that behavior.

Business coaching or consulting generally involves an initial process of assessment; then, developing solutions or recommendations, and assisting with the process of implementing those recommendations. While a business coach may have allegiance to a primary methodology, he should place the needs of the organization ahead of his preference for any one method.

TOYOTA KATA COACHING:

Mike Rother[3] has popularized a very simple model of coaching based on his experience observing how performance is improved at Toyota. It focuses on very immediate actions an individual may take to improve performance. It recommends a structured approach of asking five simple questions of the individual she is coaching. The target condition is based on a challenge, a more strategic goal, determined by a higher level of management. In one sense it is almost the opposite of life coaching which is based entirely on the agenda of the person being coached. Neither approach is wrong, they are simply based on a very different assumption about who the client is, and whose needs you are serving.

Mike Rother believes that the repetition of these questions builds the habits of performance improvement. If this process is carried out by enough individuals in an organization, it will change the culture. Rother provides the following card to coaches so they can remember to follow these questions.

COACHING KATA

The Five Questions

1) What is the **Target Condition**?
2) What is the **Actual Condition** now?

--------*(Turn Card Over)*-------------------->

3) What **Obstacles** do you think are preventing you from reaching the target condition? Which *one* are you addressing now?
4) What is your **Next Step**? (Next experiment) What do you expect?
5) How quickly can we go and see what we **Have Learned** from taking that step?

*You'll often work on the same obstacle with several experiments

Reflect on the Last Step Taken

Because you don't actually know what the result of a step will be!

1) What did you plan as your **Last Step?**
2) What did you **Expect?**
3) What **Actually Happened?**
4) What did you **Learn?**

----------------------------->
Return to question 3

(Note: the above is copied from Mike Rother's PowerPoints)

This process has value to develop the exact habits implied in these questions; however, it lacks a focus on developing teams, building more complex leadership skills, or addressing the systems and structures of an

[3] Rother, Mike. Toyota Kata, McGraw-Hill, New York, 2010.

organization that largely determine its culture. This is not a criticism, every method has its purpose and its limitations. You simply need to understand what the purpose and limitations are of each method.

In healthcare and technology organizations, such as Google, the work of teams is essential. Ideas for improvement are most likely to come from teams working together to solve problems. It is worth noting that Google's recent research on its own high performing teams found that psychological safety was the number one factor common to high performing teams. [4]

Lean Coaching:

Lean coaching incorporates the habit building process of Toyota Kata. It also seeks to develop high performing teams and team leaders. Work teams and leadership teams are at the heart of the lean culture. Teams are the first organizing unit of the organization, the first learning organization, much like the family in larger society. It is within these teams and their ability to solve problems and manage performance that the culture resides. The *lean coach* will support both the natural team leader and the team itself as they are challenged to continuously improve.

Lean coaching incorporates some aspects of all of the former coaching models. The lean coach will not only focus on immediate performance improvement, but will also assist in the development of the client's skills. By contributing to, and caring about, the client's capacity to lead, the coach creates a genuine client-centered helping relationship. At the same time, he is responsible for moving the organization toward a long-term challenge of creating lean management practices and performance. Lean coaching follows the process of coaching employed at Toyota with the purpose of creating and sustaining a lean culture.

A true lean coach will go beyond the five kata questions, although he may incorporate those, to ask the team leader whether the team has a scorecard and visual display that they review; does the team have standard work, or leader standard work, and is it being followed; is the team using a disciplined problem-solving process such as the PDCA or the A3 model? In other words, there is a great deal more to building a lean culture than the five kata questions. A lean coach will have a systems thinking view of the

---

[4] See Chapter 13 for a more in-depth discussion of this research.

organization, and she must understand that building a culture is a strategy that requires constancy of purpose over time.

What Are the Target Skills?

Coaching requires mental models of good performance. In other words, a tennis or golf coach has in mind a model of what an ideal swing looks like. A basketball coach has in mind how a defender defends against a point guard. The lean coach must have in mind an understanding of how teams and leaders solve problems and improve performance.

What skills or behavior are you helping your client to develop? These are well defined in the *Coaching Maps* you will find in Part Three of this book. These maps define the skills, the action-learning steps, and the coaching questions. These skills are taught in the *Team Kata* book and the *Team Leadership* online course. Here is a summary of those skills:

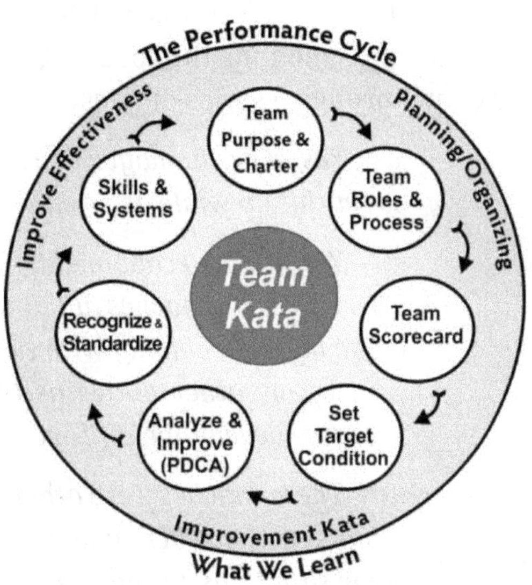

1. ***Organizing Your Team***
    a. Developing a Team Charter.
    b. Clarifying roles and responsibilities.
    c. Developing a Team Agenda.
    d. Developing a Team Scorecard and Display
2. ***Solving Problems and Improving Performance***
    a. Root Cause Analysis
    b. Brainstorming
    c. The problem solving model - Plan-Do-Check (or Study)-Act.
    d. Action Planning
    e. The A3 Problem-solving Process (see Glossary)
    f. Mapping Your Value Stream and Eliminating Waste
    g. Improving Motivation and Human Performance Problems
    h. Developing Standard Work and Leader Standard Work
3. ***Personal Effectiveness Skills***
    a. Team Facilitation Skills

b. Effective Listening
c. Giving and Receiving Feedback

Teaching these skills does not assure that they will be practiced and sustained. Coaching is the critical step that leads to adopting these skills and habits as norms in the organization.

The Toyota Way of Coaching

Dr. Jake Abraham was with Toyota for many years and was responsible for the implementing the coaching process. I asked him how this worked at Toyota through a series of questions. Here is his reply to my questions:

> *Yes, every manager at Toyota had a coach. I had the opportunity to set this up while at Toyota.*
>
> *Yes, it was economically not feasible to have coaches full time. There were no coaches full time, except there might be a master coach – like myself – helping with the development process of coaching – as part of my other duties as the continuous improvement & human resource development (Toyota Way) senior manager.*
>
> *These coaches were other next level managers – assistant general managers, general manager, vice presidents and even the president. In some situations, we had very seasoned and senior managers coaching junior managers. So part of their daily work of operational management was also to coach others.*
>
> *And, yes, it was also set up that coaching was provided by next level managers who were not their natural team leaders. It was set up as a mentee – mentor format – where a mentee might see a skill gap in a certain area within himself – and then he connects with a mentor – that has that knowledge and skill – to mentor that mentee – and help coach – mentor – close that gap. This was structurally set up where the skills of mentors were assessed and determined – and formalized – and advertised. The mentee's gaps were also assessed and determined. Pairings were then done – to ensure match with personalities too.*
>
> *So the structure would be this – each next level manager – who is a team leader for their manager – will coach their direct report managers – that is a must as part of their job – using the Toyota*

Business Practice and On the Job Development as the standard practice of coaching, plus they will coach – mentor up to 3 managers – outside their areas.

This system is also cascaded down – Managers who are immediate team leaders for their assistant managers – must coach them as part of their jobs – thru TBP and OJD as a standard practice – and these managers – will coach – mentor – up to 2 assistant managers – outside their areas. This would also include group leaders (supervisors) who would be able and capable to move laterally or upwards.

This was further cascaded down to Assistant managers and their group leaders (supervisors) – coaching as part of their job.

Hope this helps Larry

Jake

I believe that the Toyota coaching model as described above is a good model for practical and cost-effective coaching in almost any organization. Establishing this Toyota model of coaching is the goal of this book and online course.

I have always been impressed by the fact that we learn more when we teach someone else than when we are simply a student. Stephen Covey used to require students going through his Seven Habits or Principle Centered Leadership courses to learn the material and then teach it to others. Teaching others, or coaching, confirms and strengthens your own knowledge and your own appreciation for the power of a method such as the lean or team kata process. This is an integral part of how Toyota develops leaders and sustains their culture. It seems to me that this should be a feature of every lean organization.

Coaching & The Team Structure

There is a basic understanding about high performing organizations that is central to everything that follows. Everyone at Toyota is on a team. Everyone at Google is on a team. Teams are the foundational structure of any high performing organization. The senior managers are organized into teams, as are all other managers and staff. Even the Board of Directors is a team. How teams function will define the performance of the organization. If teams are focused on critical performance measures, those measures are likely to improve. If teams engage their members in problem-solving and decision-making, employees will feel engaged. If teams are engaged in continuous improvement, they will find innovations in both product and process. So, let us examine the team structure, and how coaches are going to work with the leaders of those teams.

The Development of Team Management

In the late 1970's this author was working to improve productivity and the culture of companies in the textile industry, 3M and other large organizations. This was before the quality movement, and before anyone was talking about Japanese management. We began by teaching supervisors to *"catch someone doing something good today"* to reinforce good performance, and create a less punitive environment.[5] We soon had each supervisor meeting once a week, for about a half-hour, with his shift crew. This became the *team meeting* and what we called *Team Management.* We were very data oriented so we had the team leader graph a few key data variables and share the graph with the employee team. We had not learned about the Schewhart or Deming Cycle (Plan-Do-Check-Act). We simply had the supervisor (now called the team leader) ask the team members what they thought they could do to improve performance. They would then try that improvement and see what happened. We didn't know it at the time, but we were practicing an essential component of lean management or the Toyota Production System.

We learned two other key lessons in the '70s and '80s. You could not successfully sustain a change in behavior at one level of the organization. Cultures are vertically integrated. The supervisor had to be on his department manager's team, and they had to practice the same behavior. The department managers had to be on the plant manager's team, etc. The other lesson was that without frequent coaching, over a period of many months, the new behavior was not likely to become habitual, or normal. It became our standard practice implementing *Team Management* to train internal coaches to work with all team leaders and teams. This method proved successful in dozens of organizations over a long period of time.

---

[5] The "we" in this case are this author and the consultants at what was then called Behavioral Systems, Inc. and later the Miller-Howard Consulting Group.

What we did not know was that this was very similar to the process of training and improvement at Toyota.

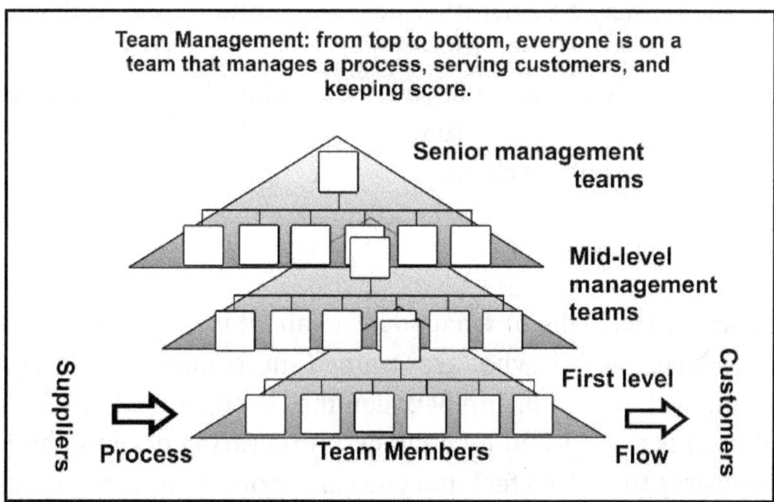

As the quality movement began, and as this author became involved at Honda in Marysville, Ohio, we continually refined our methods of problem-solving, process improvement, team effectiveness and coaching. All of this experience went into the process described in this book, as well as my *Team Kata* and *Getting to Lean* books.

THE CONTINUUM OF CARING

> *"Coaching is not so much a methodology as it is a relationship - a particular kind of relationship. Yes, there are skills to learn and a wide variety of tools available, but the real art of effective coaching comes from the coach's ability to work within the context of relationship."*[6]

The *Lean Coach* should be clear about his or her zone of caring. Is the focus on individual development, the development of teams, or on changing the architecture of the organization - the systems and structure? They are all important. But the assignment must be clear.

There are numerous ways to describe the continuum of relationships between coach and client: from short-term to long-term, from focused on today's problems to developing strategic systems and culture. For the sake

---

[6] Kimsey-House, Henry & Karen, Sandahl, Phillip and Whitworth, Laurel. Co-Active Coaching. Nicholas Brealey Publishing, Boston, 2011. P. 15..

of simplicity, I will divide this continuum into three zones: Blue, Green and Red Zones of Caring.

Although you may be operating predominantly in one of these zones along the continuum, you will find that they often overlap. They are also additive, not mutually exclusive. If you are a highly skilled coach operating in the Red Zone, you may also function in the Blue and Green Zones in response to the needs of the client.

Why Caring Matters

If you are a coach, who or what you care about is central to your ability to affect change. Those who are trained in counseling or coaching understand that the relationship between the coach and client is based on trust, and trust is established by demonstrating caring or empathy for the client. The degree to which I feel that you care about *me* and *my* success will determine the degree to which I am likely to share my own concerns and follow your advice. If the focus of the coach is outside of the client, on the needs of someone else, there is little reason to expect the client to accept responsibility for self-reflection or change.

Relationships are highly intuitive and they are based on far more than the simple words spoken or questions asked. Clients have an intuitive sense of the motivation of the coach. A coach without self-awareness of his or her own motivations is not likely to build a trusting relationship with the client.

1. The Blue Zone: Individual Habits

Some coaching focuses entirely on habits that impact the performance of the organization. While developing these habits may contribute to performance, there are many other drivers of the culture not addressed by this method. Some coaching in this zone is driven by the needs of the organization and not the needs of the individual.

There are a couple obvious limitations to Blue Zone coaching. First, it demonstrates a superficial caring for the individual client. It is not about the person, but about habits of improving performance. The focus is on the "object" of performance, not the complexity of the person or of the organization's culture. There is a top down assumption that the challenge is set at a higher level of management, assuring that it is not the client's needs but the needs of the organization that are being addressed. By definition then, it is not about what is important to the client, but what is important to someone else. The focus is also on improving short-term performance and not the nature of the organization's structures, systems, and capabilities that will ultimately determine long-term performance.

2. The Green Zone: Teams and Processes

Every family therapist has experienced Mom or Dad bringing Johnny to therapy because there is something "wrong" with him. Johnny is misbehaving, he is broken, please fix him! It doesn't take long for the therapist to discover that Johnny's behavior is perfectly rational given the system in which he lives. We all adapt to the system in which we live, and a crazy system produces crazy behavior as viewed by an outsider. You can't fix Johnny without fixing the family system, the behavior of Mom and Dad.

Organizations are like family systems. It is the first learning organization, the group of people on whom we depend the most and who depend on us. It is the group to which we belong, the team, whether the

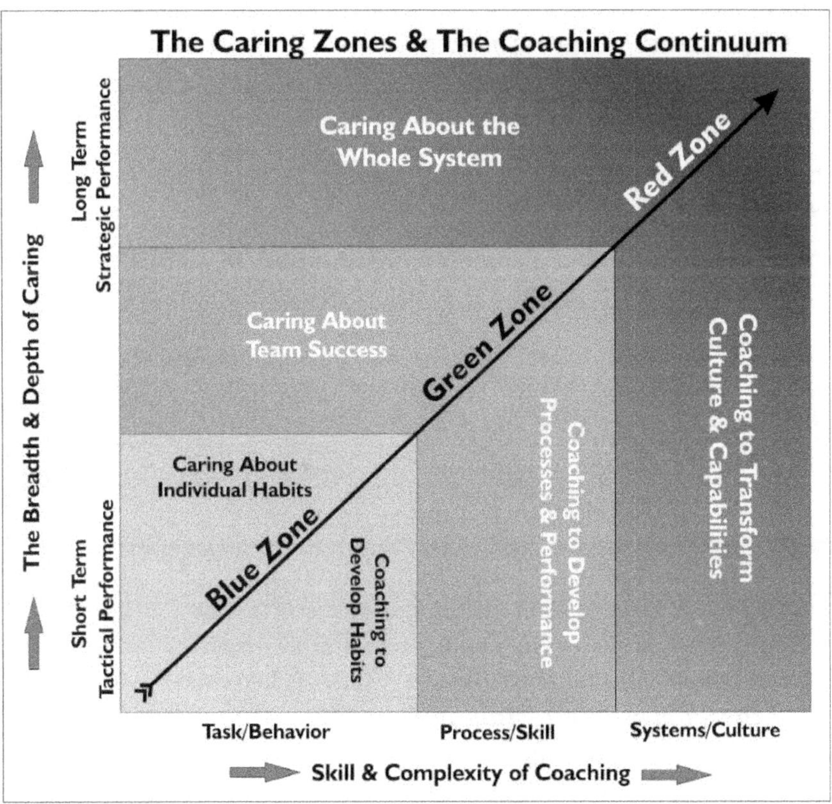

senior management team or the front line team doing the value-adding work. The functioning of this team is the key to the functioning of the entire organization. You can't improve the performance of the organization without improving the behavior and norms of the natural work teams and leadership teams.

There is some confusion about the nature of work teams. While there has been a lot written about self-managed, or self-directed teams, having implemented team systems and trained teams for many years, I can definitely say that there is no such thing as a totally self-directed or self-managing team. The senior management team is directed by the owners of the organization, and every team below receives direction, and operates within boundaries determined at the level above. However, teams may still be empowered and self-directed within those boundaries. The nature of self-direction, the team's boundaries, is entirely dependent on the context, the nature of work done by those teams, as well as their training and leadership.

Coaching these teams requires a set of skills and a different relationship than coaching individuals to improve immediate performance. It requires observing patterns of group behavior, helping to define roles and responsibilities, and it is here that the problem-solving skills and process mapping are most useful. It is the *team kata* (discipline of practice) more than the individual kata that will determine both the culture and the performance of the organization.

Coaching teams requires a deep understanding of facilitation skills and group dynamics. It also requires the ability to give feedback to a number of different levels of leaders in the organization.

The team is the transition structure between the individual and the culture of the organization so the coach must now demonstrate caring not only for the individual but for the team as a whole, the family unit. She must observe and give feedback to the entire team. And, rather than the five repetitive questions of the Toyota Kata, she needs to move the team and its leaders up a skills hierarchy. The skills of team leadership are more complex than the Kata questions address. I have attempted to provide a definition of the skills, actions, and the coaching questions in my *Team Kata Coaching Map (see the Part Three of this book).* This is one way of defining this complexity.

3. The Red Zone: Whole-System Change

Great athletic coaches, particularly at the high school and college level, are not only concerned with the specific skills that lead to success on the field or court. Duke University's legendary basketball coach, Coach K (Mike Krzyzewski) often talks about the importance of developing his players as "men", well-functioning human beings, both on and off the court. He has won the NCAA Championship five times. His focus on the whole person does not diminish his success at teaching the fundamentals of basketball.

The Red Zone has two dimensions, one is the personal concern for the development of the whole individual and the other is an understanding of the whole-system of the organization. Coaching to improve each of these require both a relevant mental framework, and a set of facilitation skills.

Addressing the organization as a whole-system requires a different set of skills and a different model of change. Socio-technical systems design, or what I have called *Whole System Architecture,* provides a conceptual model and a process of change, which I have detailed in my *Getting to Lean* book. Of course there are other frameworks that can be employed. However, the framework must address the systems of the organization such as who gets what information, who makes what decisions, how does the structure support the flow of the work, and whether the capabilities of the organization match the changing requirements imposed by the external landscape.

Toyota in Japan, in the 1990's, had a turnover rate of 25% among newly hired workers, and they were running out of workers. They realized that there was something dramatically wrong with their system. Along with their union, they redesigned their own system to the degree that one writer claimed that Toyota had abandoned lean manufacturing altogether. They had not abandoned it, but their previous focus on the technical system alone had created misalignment with the needs of people who worked within that system, and they had to redesign the essential nature of the work process to align the social and technical systems.

We have been introduced to many problem-solving models as the solution to all ills. Whether it is Six-Sigma's DCMAIC, or the Shewart Cycle of PDCA, or the A3 problem-solving model (see Glossary), they are all predicated on the idea that there is a specific problem to be solved. Why do you think there are so many problems? Could it be that there is something more fundamentally wrong?

Problems are within the current state system. Transformational change is not problem-solving. It is designing the whole-system to meet the needs of all stakeholders, internal and external. It is also about adaptation to both the current and future external environment. It is an act of creating something, not fixing something.

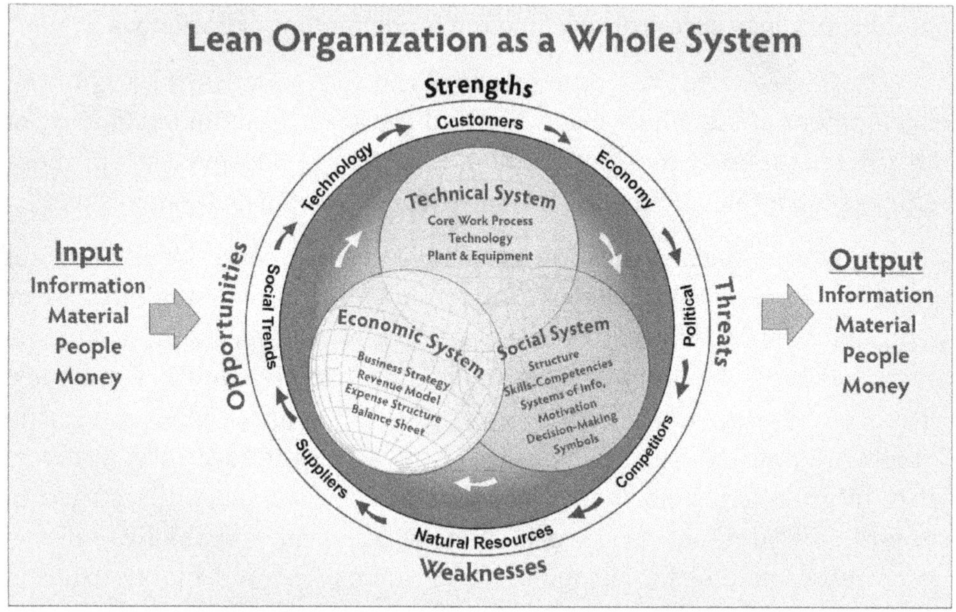

Transformational change is about pro-actively creating the future organization based on the threats and opportunities presented by the external environment. It asks, "Given the future environment, the technology, the market and social changes, what do we need to be like in the future and how do we create that future?" It is designing a fundamentally different house than the one we are living in. Yes, there is a "problem", but you won't find the problem by fixing every symptom.

Transformational change is a process designed to create significant change in the culture and work processes of an organization and produce significant improvement in performance. If you need to align your organization and its culture to your strategy, you need whole-system design. If the organization creates walls and barriers to the flow of work, you need whole-system design. If the market place is changing significantly and your organization needs to respond to changing technologies, customer demands, or regulation, you need whole-system design.

The nature of this process and these issues are entirely different from those that address individual habits or the patterns of team behavior. They are analogous to a nation's tax laws and system of investment and spending, versus a local community's governance. Too many change efforts that are presented as efforts to change the culture fail to address the systems and structures that reinforce the existing culture.

Chapter 2

The Coach's Roles and Responsibilities

The purpose of the Lean Coach is to develop the skills of leaders and teams so they may succeed at continuous improvement. Implementing a lean culture requires a change in habit patterns and the coach's job is to aid in training and reinforcing this development.

These skills and habits must be acquired through an *action-learning* sequence that includes a) knowledge acquisition; b) practice; c) feedback; d) more practice and, e) positive reinforcement that encourages further use of the new skill. This is best done in small steps over time. In the ideal world every team and team leader would be coached by their manager. However, managers are often too busy, and may not have the skills to provide this coaching. It is for this reason that it is desirable to identify internal lean coaches who can provide coaching to both managers and teams.

A lean coach has several roles and responsibilities. The first is, of course, to coach his or her own team. Then, the Lean Coach has the additional responsibility of assisting in the development of other team leaders.

What responsibilities does the coach accept in this role? One is to facilitate the learning process. This does not mean that the coach provides the training. Today, the most efficient way to provide training is online, at the learners pace, on any device, anywhere. The coach can suggest an appropriate pace of learning and debrief with the student as they complete sections of the course. The second major responsibility is to directly observe the learners' behavior, meet with them and establish goals, and follow-up to discuss their progress. Providing feedback and encouragement is essential to being a good coach. This second responsibility is often the more difficult because the coach must learn to influence in the absence of power. The coach must overcome his or her own natural hesitancy to give honest feedback. Support by a Master Coach or a senior executive change champion is often helpful in this respect.

The Role of the Lean Coach:

- The coach will facilitate training in a sequence that guides the team leader and teams through their development.
- The coach will meet with the team leader to plan meetings and to provide feedback to the leader (the *client*) on her own leadership of the team.
- The coach will understand the current condition of their client's performance, the challenge for improvement, and contract with the client to take steps toward the desired future performance.
- The coach will "go to the Gemba" by directly observing team and leader behavior.
- The coach will participate on a team of coaches who will evaluate the process of developing teams and their leaders, and work to improve that process.

The Competencies of a Lean Coach:

- The lean coach will have knowledge of lean management and will have participated in a successful lean implementation.
- The coach should possess excellent communication skills, both the ability to effectively listen and provide feedback.
- The coach will be an effective team member herself.
- She will be well organized and able to plan meetings effectively.
- He will be respected by his peers for his ability to work well with others.

- She will be humble in her presentation, yet forthright and honest in her willingness to give her opinion on the progress of the group and its members.

Blended Learning: The New Model for Developing Leadership Skills

We learn with all of our senses. We listen, we read, we watch, we explore and practice, we receive feedback from a coach, and we finally become fluent in new skills. Blended learning assumes that no one mode of learning will result in the adoption of new patterns of thought or behavior. It assumes a *learning system* that employs multiple forms of learning over an extended period of time.

Developing effective coaches is best done by using a cascading learning model. It is desirable to have an experienced coach who has led a change process and coached teams successfully in the past. This *Master Coach* is the mentor to a trainee coach. She provides a role model, and models desired pinpointed behavior for the *Trainee Coach*. This Master Coach is skilled at pinpointing the exact behavior that comprises the skill of effective coaching (more on this in a later chapter). The Trainee Coach then facilitates the learning of a team leader. Again, this coach models behavior, pinpoints exactly the behavior that leads to successful team leadership, observes the team leader, and provides feedback and reinforcement. The coach will also directly observe the team as it meets to solve problems and manage their own performance. The coach then provides feedback to the team leader, indicating how he or she can improve the performance of the team.

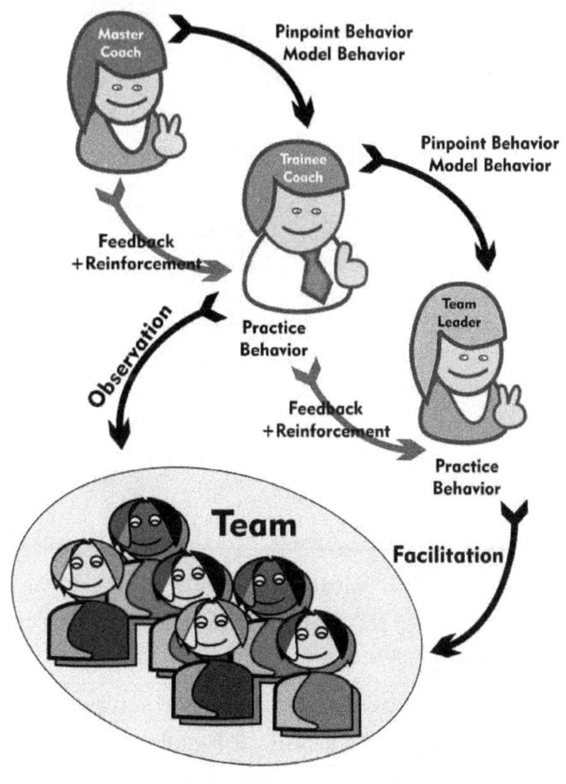

One perhaps unfortunate fact of life for many organizations is that they simply cannot afford to bring managers together for frequent training sessions in a central training location or hotel conference rooms. This has been the traditional model of training for many years and many organizations still assume that this is the best way to develop their leaders. However, technology and the Internet are changing everything, from how we communicate with family members, how we do our banking, and how we learn new skills.

There is a generation gap in regard to how individuals expect to learn new skills. The baby-boom generation expected their manager to plan training events, and they would dutifully sit through a three-day workshop

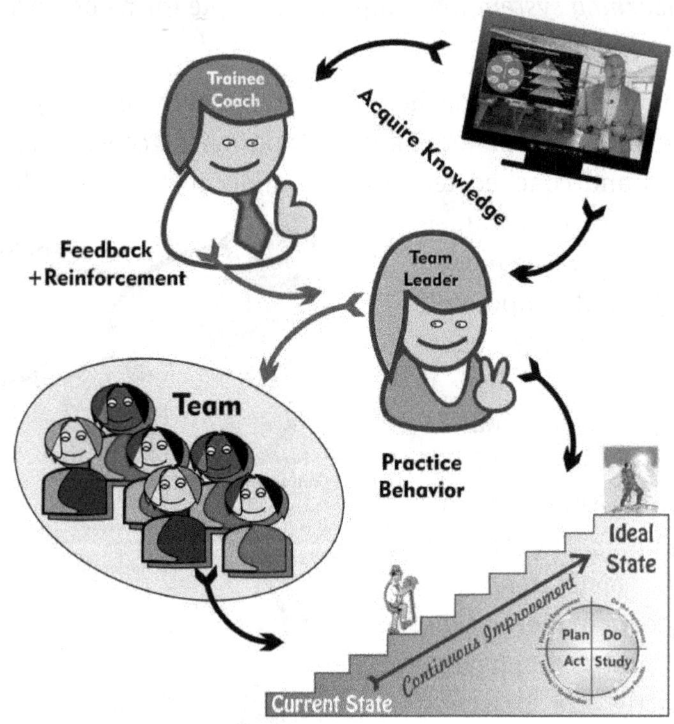

and be glad when it was over. Millennials (born between 1982 and 2004) and Generation Xers (born 1960- early '80s) have grown up Googling anything that pops into their mind, discovering YouTube videos, online courses, or Wikipedia articles on any subject. Generation Xers may be found sitting at Starbucks staring at their iPads, and while you may think they are reading their email or Facebook page, they may also be online watching a lecture on how to develop an IOS10 iPhone app. Time and place are less relevant with 24/7 access to training.

The action-learning process recommended in this book is very much like the PDSA problem-solving model in that it is a cycle of learning through experimentation.

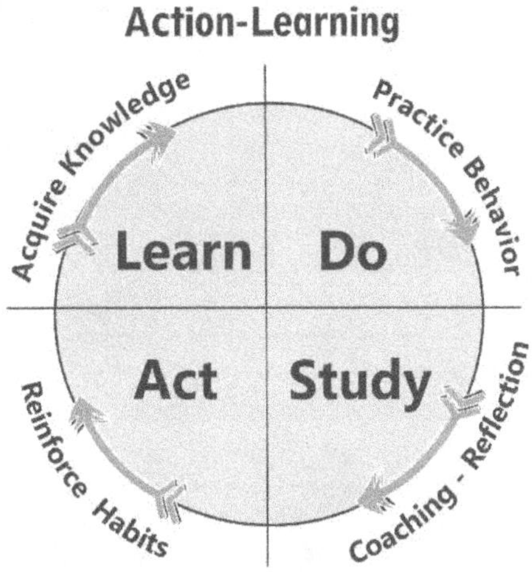

Knowledge acquisition is the easiest part of acquiring a skill. For example, you can easily discover online, that certain fingers placed on certain keys form a chord on the piano keyboard. Similarly, the knowledge of the problem-solving steps, or the use of different decision styles, can be accessed anytime, anywhere, using online courses. You should not waste time and money getting a group into a workshop room to impart that knowledge. Let the learner acquire it on their time, accessing the knowledge online.

The more critical stage of learning - and this is where coaching is most helpful, is when the student practices the new behavior and receives feedback and encouragement. They learn then practice their new skills with their team. The team practices its problem-solving skills, for example, led by the team leader. They go through a sequence of continuous improvement steps, repeating the Plan-Do-Check-Act cycle, developing their skills each time. The Team Leader gives feedback to the team and the Coach gives feedback to the Team Leader.

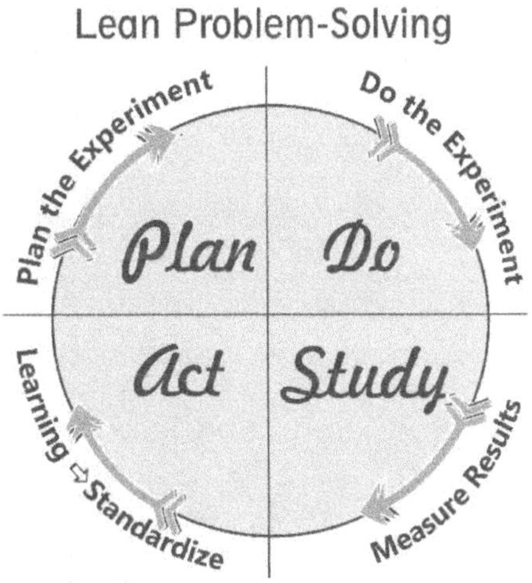

This multi-mode learning, blending different learning opportunities and styles, is unquestionably the direction for future corporate or organizational training. It employs current technology, uses internal resources in the most effective way, and quickly elicits action that leads to improved performance.

Chapter 3

Principles of Lean Coaching

There are a few basic ideas of lean management and behavior analysis that will help us understand the steps in the process of lean coaching. These are simple yet profoundly important ideas. They should be a reference point for the lean coach.

The following *principles* have proven to be central to successful lean coaching.

The Scientific Method

With the adoption of the scientific method of learning, all human progress accelerated. Major causes of death and suffering - polio, typhus, smallpox and yellow fever have been eliminated. Life expectancy in developed countries is approximately 80 years, when it was half that just two hundred years ago. Our lives have been changed for the better by the microprocessor, the computer, the Internet and a thousand other technological advances. In 2002 only ten percent of Africans owned a mobile phone. Today, approximately 80% of Africans have cell phones, 30% make and receive financial payments by phone, and can access the Internet. In other words, the majority of Africans have gained access to most of the knowledge of the human race, in just a few years. What excuse do we have for not applying the scientific method in our own process of learning?

When one hears the term *scientific method* one may visualize laboratory scientists toiling over Bunsen burners and beakers. But the application of the scientific method is not reserved for the laboratory. It is a very practical, simple and easily understood thing. Consider that the entire Toyota Production System has been created on the idea of applying the scientific method to all activities, by all employees.

What exactly is the scientific method? Very simply, *it is a method of answering questions or gaining knowledge by observation, measurement and conducting experiments that may then be replicated.* It is studying the cause and effect relationships between two variables by observing and measuring that effect. In other words, every time you cook a meal and try some new ingredient, then taste the effect of that new ingredient, you are doing an experiment, using the scientific method. Anytime you try a new procedure, a change in the work process, and you have measured the performance of that process before, and then after the change, you are using the scientific method. Of course, there are many degrees of scientific rigor, discipline of data analysis and replicability. However, in most work settings, and for most improvements, a relatively simple level of scientific analysis is sufficient.

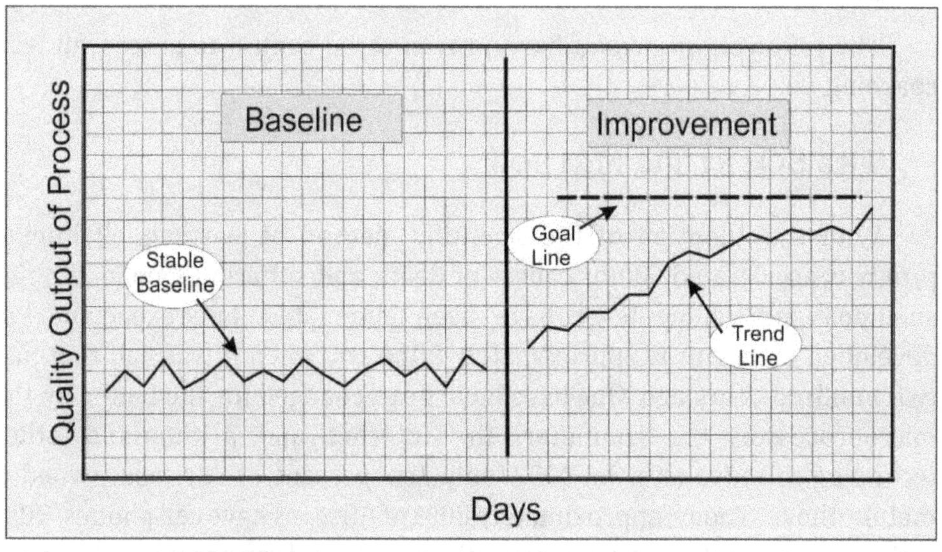

If you are using the scientific method, the first thing you do is "know the facts" as Dr. Deming used to say. You get the data on the current, or *baseline* performance. Without this baseline data it is impossible to know whether any change has been effective. It is best to make a change in a process when you have a stable baseline. If the baseline data is in an upward trend you will not know whether your change caused improvement or whether it was headed that way anyway.

If you are using the scientific method, you do your best to make only one change at a time. You control the variables – the number of things that might affect the data. If you make five changes to a process at the same time and performance improves, you will not know which change had the desired effect. Some of the changes might have had a negative effect, but you will not be able to separate the causes of change.

And, most importantly, you have to watch the data to gain understanding. High performing teams are data-focused. The leader and coach must help the team gain this understanding.

THE CHALLENGE

A life well lived is not a life of ease. On the contrary, it is a life motivated by the pursuit of a challenge, a worthy purpose. *Creative dissatisfaction* is the condition of knowing the challenge, where or who you wish to be, and, knowing the gap between the current state and that ideal state you are seeking. The challenge is to close that gap, and this is the most essential form of motivation.

What is the role of leaders in an organization? It is not to solve every problem or to create a condition of ease. It is to define the strategic challenge for the organization, and to help others set targets that move incrementally toward that challenge.

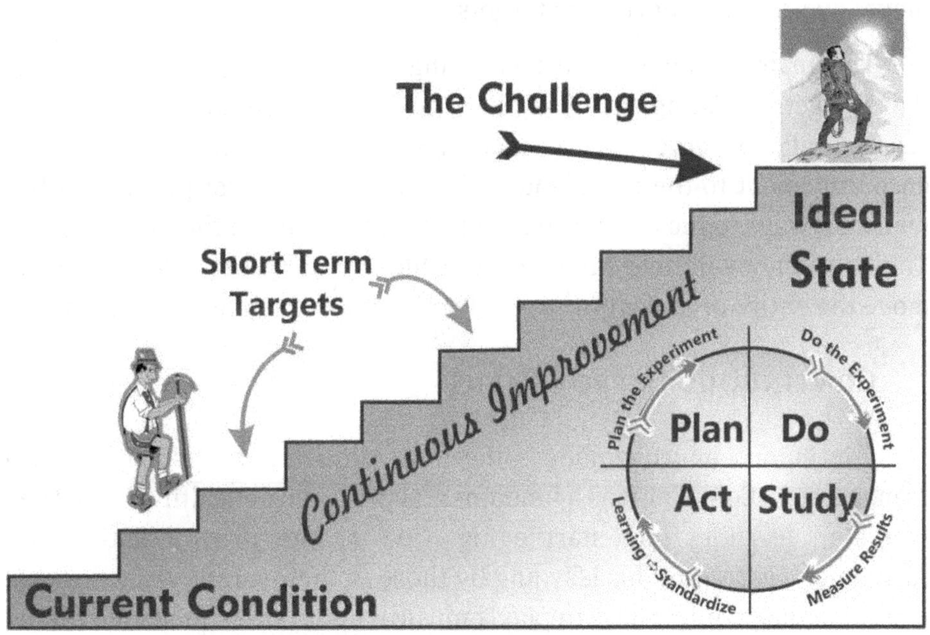

Setting objectives, targets, or goals has been a subject of voluminous research and writing over the past fifty years. Dr. Deming advocated "eliminating Management by Objectives." His objection with management by objectives was the too often autocratic, top-down, nature of objective setting. This is where the distinction between a long-term challenge and short-term target conditions, or performance, can be helpful. The long-term challenge is determined by the strategy of the organization – understanding the strategic changes in markets, technology, the economy, etc. To survive, every business must understand the threats and opportunities presented by the external environment and develop strategic intent – the direction, the challenge in order to grow and survive. Short-term targets that move toward that challenge are a very different thing. Every team should continually be setting short-term achievable targets that represent continuous improvement toward the strategic challenge.

For example, a manufacturing organization may recognize that they need to reduce costs and increase manufacturing efficiency by 25% over the next two years. This is a significant challenge. Each team in the manufacturing plant cannot own this goal. But, they can identify specific and more immediate targets to improve the run rate, or efficiency on the specific machine or operation for which they are responsible. To achieve this, they can daily employ the PDCA (Plan Do Check Act) cycle of problem-solving to move toward their short-term targets.

The team leader will be facilitating the problem-solving to achieve these targets, assisting with compiling the data and displaying that data. The coach will observe team meetings and provide feedback and encouragement to the team leader. She may also suggest problem-solving methods, ways to include more members of the team in the discussion, etc. Together, they will help the team to achieve their short-term targets and move the entire organization toward achieving the strategic challenge.

Continuous Improvement

Continuous improvement is the most fundamental principle of lean management. Consider it as a fundamental principle of healthy living. When you stop learning you start aging. One of the proven antidotes to Alzheimer's is continuous learning by those in their senior years. Learning a new language or learning to play a musical instrument keeps the brain in a healthy state. The brain is much like a muscle that when not used atrophies and becomes weak.

Companies and teams are similar. They are healthy and grow by seeking continuous improvement. Teams can engage in continuous improvement when they have the data on their performance, know the challenge, set targets, and plan experiments to improve their performance. This should never end! This can't be emphasized enough. Lean management or continuous improvement is a never ending process. The job of the coach is to help instill this understanding among all team members, and provide the means to succeed in setting targets and continuously improving.

Shaping Behavior

The idea of shaping behavior is something that every parent and teacher does, perhaps intuitively. The coach should be conscious and think through the shaping sequence. *Shaping behavior is the process of reinforcing successive approximations to a terminal behavior or skill.* In other words, if you are learning to play acoustic blues guitar, you do not start by attempting to learn a complex tune in its entirety. Rather, you start by just practicing the alternating, steady thumb pattern on the sixth and fourth strings. This is the drum beat, the rhythm section of almost every blues piece. You then practice adding a few notes with the index finger. Then you practice a roll, a sequence of thumb and finger picks. You practice those until they become almost automatic.

What you are doing in this sequence, and what every good instructor does, is break down the skill into its component behaviors. Help the student learn one simple behavior, reinforce that behavior, then move on to another behavior. Eventually you will chain these behaviors together into a fluid flow, skill fluency. This fluency is the mark of every good athlete and every musician. It is also the mark of a great team leader.

How does the coach shape behavior? She observes the team and team leader in a meeting, and takes note of those behaviors that result in effective facilitation and problem-solving, and of those that do not. She then coaches the team leader by pointing out just one or two simple things that he could do better. At a subsequent meeting the coach again observes and provides recognition, positive reinforcement, for the successful performance of those behaviors. The coach then suggests one or two other behaviors that might improve the team meeting. The sequence is repeated as the skill of facilitation becomes more and more fluent.

Action Learning

Lean management is not simply about learning. It is about doing and performing. It is about implementing a new way of managing the organization. This book and associated training are designed to elicit new behavior on the part of managers and teams.

It is important that you manage the process of implementation. That means that there should be clear expectations in terms of what each team will do to implement the lean process. The *Coaching Maps* (see Part 3 of this book) illustrate the sequence of course lectures, action steps, and coaching questions. The action steps are "deliverables," things that a team will do to demonstrate their learning and to improve their functioning as a team. The complete maps can be downloaded within the online course.

Some of the chapters do not have an associated deliverable. That is because they are focused on learning skills and improving relationships within the team. Effective facilitation skills are essential, but the deliverable is simply improved decision-making and problem-solving.

It will be helpful if the coach tracks the training modules and deliverables completed for each team. This can be done on an Excel spreadsheet, as illustrated on the following page. This will help motivate the team and keep them on track in their development.

The twenty-five items listed on the below Excel spreadsheet are auditable deliverables that are completed as a team progresses through their training. These action items are the implementation of the team kata process for any given team.

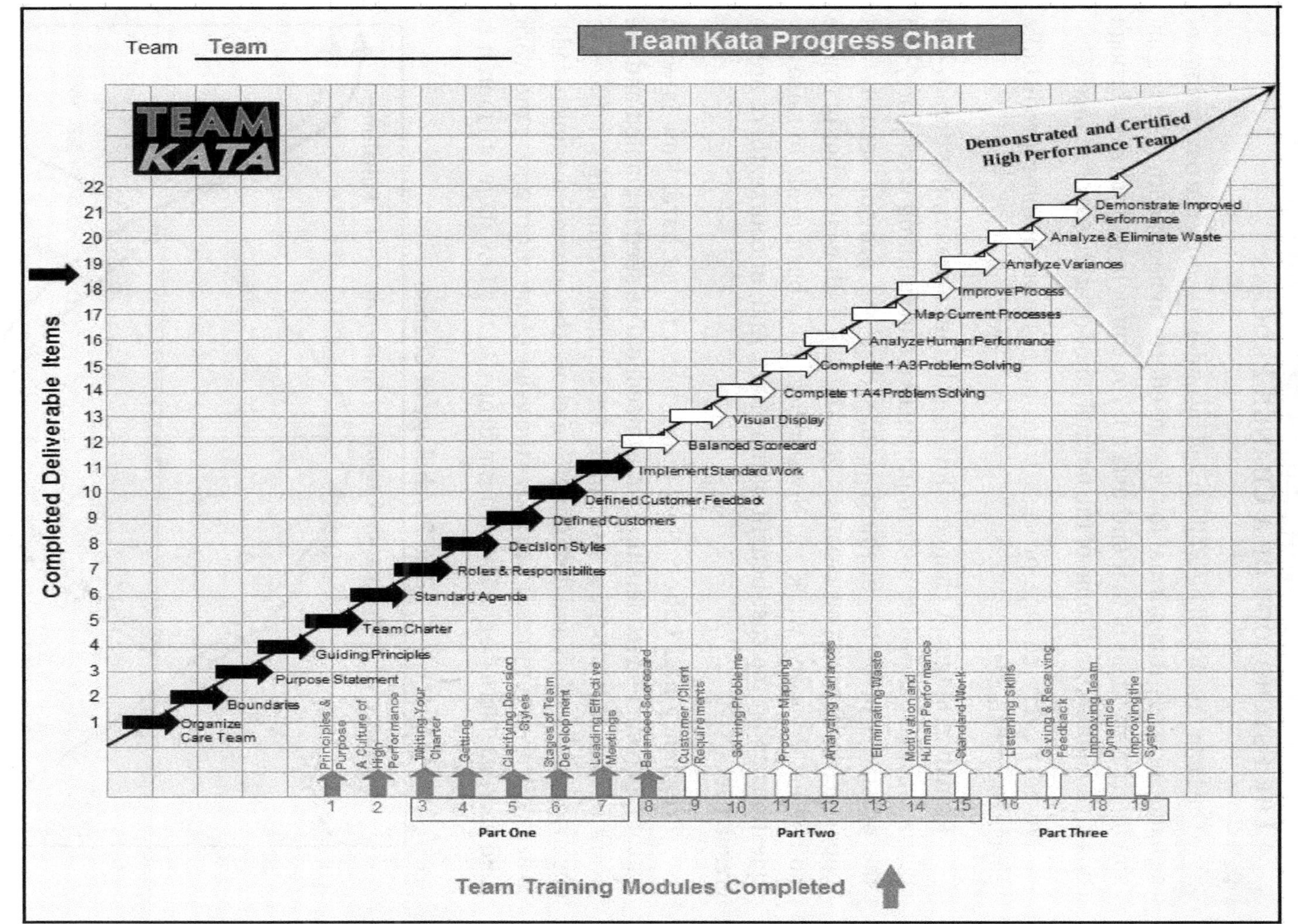
Team Team
Team Kata Progress Chart
TEAM KATA
Completed Deliverable Items
22
21
20
19
18
17
16
15
14
13
12
11
10
9
8
7
6
5
4
3
2
1
Organize Care Team
Boundaries
Purpose Statement
Guiding Principles
Team Charter
Standard Agenda
Roles & Responsibilites
Decision Styles
Defined Customers
Defined Customer Feedback
Implement Standard Work
Balanced Scorecard
Visual Display
Complete 1 A4 Problem Solving
Complete 1 A3 Problem Solving
Analyze Human Performance
Map Current Processes
Improve Process
Analyze Variances
Analyze & Eliminate Waste
Demonstrate Improved Performance
Demonstrated and Certified High Performance Team
Principles & Purpose
A Culture of High Performance
Writing Your Charter
Getting
Clarifying Decision Styles
Stages of Team Development
Leading Effective Meetings
Balanced Scorecard
Customer /Client Requirements
Solving Problems
Process Mapping
Analyzing Variances
Eliminating Waste
Motivation and Human Performance
Standard Work
Listening Skills
Giving & Receiving Feedback
Improving Team Dynamics
Improving the System
1
2
3
4
5
6
7
8
9
10
11
12
13
14
15
16
17
18
19
Part One
Part Two
Part Three
Team Training Modules Completed

The Psychology of a Change Process

The Lean Coach will be well served by understanding the psychology of a change process. It is normal for change efforts to begin with enthusiasm, and then suffer a loss of that enthusiasm. You can help your clients through this if you understand some of the normal emotional stages of change.

Almost every change process transitions through some predictable psychological stages.

Romance Stage: A change effort is sold on a dream, the dream of a better way, an easier life, a more productive and fulfilling workplace, and the prospects of better business results that will provide security and opportunities for all. This creates a good deal of enthusiasm, but of course no one has done any work yet. No sacrifices have been made to raise any questions about the cost-benefit of the effort. And, of course, there are no results yet.

Pregnancy and Labor: Now things begin to get hard. Now is when encouragement and leadership is most needed. The seed is planted and the work of growth has begun, stretching our capacity, requiring sacrifices to be made, extra effort and discipline. Somehow, the romance begins to fade. There still aren't any results to prove the value of the effort, and as the work and sacrifice increase the enthusiasm drops. In the last stage of labor, it is

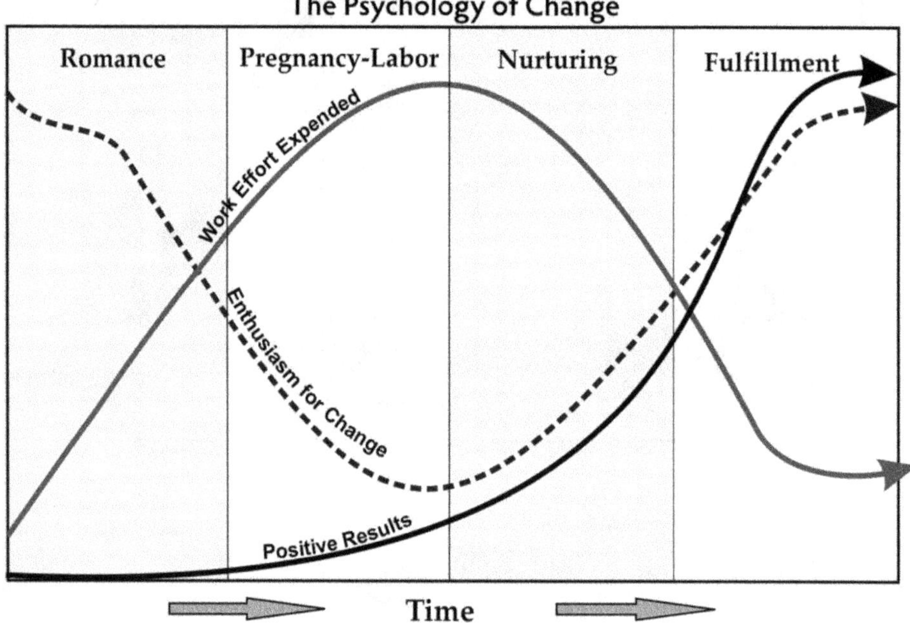

normal to see one party snapping at the other, saying something like "how could you do this to me?!! Whose dumb idea was this?"

Nurturing: A point comes when the effort begins to bear fruit, the infant emerges smiling, screaming and pooping. With basic patterns of behavior and skills established, the effort is not so difficult anymore. There is an acceptance of the process, and the first signs of actual results begin to appear. There is still the need for coaching, training, encouragement and discipline. But, it begins to be less difficult, and the early results begin to renew some enthusiasm.

Fulfillment: The group begins to achieve *mastery*, the skill and knowledge to perform are now established, and a *flow* begins to be achieved. Results are now increasing in frequency, and a critical mass of employees is experiencing these results. A tipping point is now achieved when enthusiasm increases, the effort is much less hard, and the results are proving the value of the effort. Now most people admit that they actually are the parents of this idea, after all. But, like all good things, it will still require effort and discipline to maintain.

United We Succeed!

The principle of unity is one of the first principles of performance. It is recognized by every general of every army. It is recognized by every coach of every sports team. It applies to families, communities, countries, companies and work teams.

The progress of the human race can be seen as the progress of increasing circles of unity from the family to tribe, to city state and religion, to nations and global alliances and global culture.

Why do we say "she has her act together?" "Wow is he coming unglued." "I hope he doesn't fall apart!" "I am feeling very disconnected." "She is out of touch." "Get it together, man!" In our popular culture we intuitively recognize the value of connections versus fragmentation. Intuitively we know that someone who is "together" will perform better than someone who is "falling apart." Unity of self, unity of groups, unity of companies or countries, results in superior performance.

So, what are the implications of this principle when building a lean culture? Do it all together; top to bottom in the organization. The worst mistake in managing change is to say, "Well, those folks need it more than anyone else, so let's start there." That will guarantee failure. "Those folks" will resist like the devil because they will resent being singled out as the problem group.

Some years ago I initiated a team process at Delmarva Power and Light in Wilmington, Delaware. During my first visit I met with Nev Curtis, then the CEO of the company. As we talked about how to increase the probability of success of the desired change I said "If you want this to succeed you need to be the model, you need to do it yourself, and do it first." He replied, absolutely, my team needs to be Team #1. And they were. They participated in exactly the same training and went through the same steps in building their team as everyone else in the organization. Delmarva Power and Light became a model of quality management, and their team process was the heart of their effort.

Chapter 4

Who are Your Clients & What Are Their Needs?

One of the first things that any consultant or coach should clarify is "Who are my clients and what are their goals and needs?"

Coaching is a helping relationship. If the coach is to be successful, he or she must develop a trusting and transparent relationship with the client. It must be clear who you are reporting to, what information you will and will not share, and what degree of confidentiality will you have with each person.

Take a look at the diagram below. It represents a typical set of relationships for a Lean Coach. The coach will normally have a reporting relationship to a senior manager and will be coaching a subordinate manager. The manager, or team leader, has a formal reporting relationship to the senior manager. The senior manager should also be coaching the

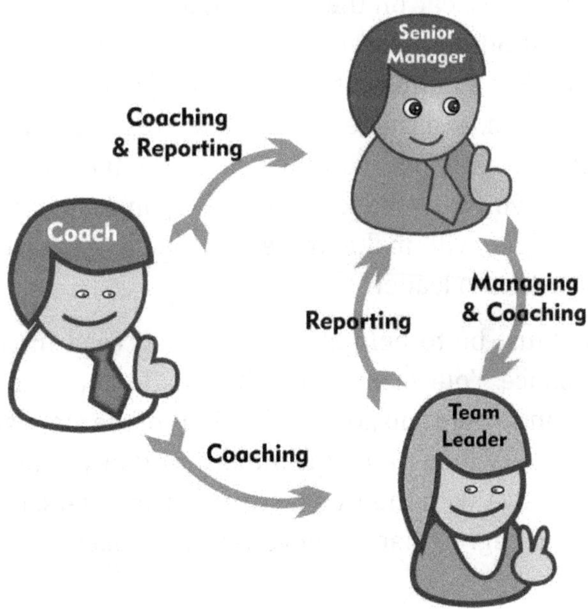

team leader as a permanent responsibility of his job. The coach may have a temporary relationship with the team leader and/or with the senior manager. They are both his clients and he has a responsibility to both.

Given this typical set of relationships, the coach should ask herself the following questions:

- What information do I share with the senior manager? Do I share all information on the behavior and progress of the team leader?
- Does the team leader know what information I will share with the senior manager?
- Does the senior manager expect you to give him feedback or advice on how he is or should be managing the team leader?
- Is your primary responsibility to help the team leader succeed or is it to help the senior manager succeed?
- If the team leader asks you to keep some information confidential, are you comfortable doing that and will this be acceptable to the senior manager? What type of information might be confidential and what may not be confidential?
- What role do ethics play in this set of relationships?

There is more than one right answer to these questions. What is most important is that you are clear on the answers, and they have been agreed to by all parties. What often causes problems is a misunderstanding about these relationships. For example, if the senior manager expects you to report everything to him, and the team leader shares information that she thinks will be held in confidence, you then share the information with the senior manager and you now have what the team leader regards as a violation of trust. This will make it very difficult to have a helping relationship with that team leader.

Your purpose must be to help all parties to succeed in continuously improving performance. Your primary loyalty should not be to the success of a program. Programs come and go. But, the skills of the manager and team leader will last for a very long time. It is important that you sincerely view them as individuals, each with their own struggles and fears. I will listen to you as a coach, to the degree that I believe you are sincerely trying to help me.

If the client feels that she is being asked to help the coach, the relationship is entirely different and unlikely to succeed. The client is most likely to adopt new behavior and continue that behavior if she feels it is in her interest, rather than in the interest of the coach.

Intention is important. Intention has power in itself. If one is trying to *act* in a helpful way, but without the sincere intention of helping the client, it is extremely difficult to succeed in this *acting*. Developing sincerity in your desire to be of service, to help your client, is the first challenge for the coach. Then the coach must begin to consider how he or she may be helpful to the team leader. What is the need of the team leader? This is the beginning of developing a helping relationship between the coach and client.

What Are Your Client's Needs?

The beginning of any successful coach/client relationship is to understand your client's needs. It is useful to use the Needs Analysis on the following page. This will help you and the client develop a shared understanding of the relationship and shared goals. It is also useful to prioritize these needs. Establishing these priorities with the client will be the beginning of a successful relationship.

You may have a team leader as client as well as a sponsoring, more senior manager. It may be useful to have the team leader recognize the needs of the senior manager, as well as the reverse. This "gets everyone on the same page" in terms of your role and expectations.

Client Needs Analysis			
Who are Your Clients?	What are their stated needs?	What can I do to help meet their needs?	Priority A, B, or C

A. Engage Your Client in the Process:

You will succeed as a coach to the degree that your client feels ownership of the change. Your job is to help your client feel in control, feel that her needs are being met, and feel that she is giving direction and providing leadership to the process.

Real engagement is having actual power to make decisions. No one will feel engaged for long if they do not, in fact, have the ability to make decisions and guide a change process.

This is true for both your client manager and for the team you may be coaching. It is more important that they both feel in control than that they follow some predetermined script or plan.

How are you going to do this?

First you need to establish a regular pattern of consultations, meetings between you and your client, whether manager or team.

Empathy and Understanding:

If we feel that someone has little understanding of our situation and cannot appreciate our feelings, we are most likely to resist their assistance. The ability to empathize with a client has long been understood as an essential component of a helping relationship. This applies to coaching team leaders just as it does to other helping relationships.

Everyone has a "problem." The coach has the problem of developing each team and causing the formal team leader to lead the team in a productive direction. You know what your problem is. But, do you know what the team leader's problem is? What are they concerned about? Only if you understand their concerns and can empathize with those concerns can you begin to help the team leader to move a positive direction and adopt new behavior.

Imagine that you are beginning an interview with your client. Generally, a client/coach meeting begins with small talk – a simple conversation to break the ice. But this small talk can be a way of beginning to understand what is on the mind of the client.

Opening Questions: What are some questions that you might ask your client to begin the conversation? These questions should be nonthreatening and contain no challenge or the appearance of an "agenda" on your part. But, listen carefully to the client's response, and see if you begin to hear what is on his or her mind. You can then begin to express empathy or understanding for the concerns of the client.

____

____

____

____

Sensing Questions: After these initial questions, what questions might you ask to bring the conversation closer to the process of continuous improvement? These questions might refer to the previous meeting and the agreements regarding target performance and the pinpointed behavior you are seeking to improve.

____

____

____

____

It is now important that you express understanding or empathy with your client. Put yourself in his or her shoes and try to understand his or her feelings from the perspective of the team leader.

Remember the models for making empathy statements:

"I can understand that... (the situation)... may cause you to feel... (a word like 'worried', or 'upset') "

"It sounds like you feel... (a feeling word like 'upset')... because... (the reason)."

"It must be ... (feeling work like "difficult, or painful")...when ... (the circumstance causing the difficulty).

Now practice the sequence of asking an open-ended question about the functioning of the team, or the team leader's role.

Planning Your Coaching Meetings

You should have a regularly scheduled meeting with your client. This should be an agreed upon part of your relationship. What you should not do is wait until there is a problem or crisis requiring your intervention. If you do this, your meeting will automatically be viewed in a negative light.

At the beginning of the team process you might meet once a week or every other week. After a couple months you might reduce this to once a month. In your first meeting with your client you might suggest a regular agenda for your meetings and a regular schedule of meetings. Your meets should be guided by the coaching model presented in the following chapter. What should be on the agenda? The following are among the possible topics:

1. **Review the Facts**: What are the facts of the key data variables. What is the current condition both in regard to performance measures and your observation of the behavior of the team?
2. **Recognition:** Be sure to celebrate the progress of your client.
3. **Pinpoint Behavior:** How do you feel the team is performing in terms of the team process? Are they an effective team? What behavior indicates either their effectiveness or problems? How can these improve?
4. **Action Plan Review:** What commitments were made in previous meetings between you and your client, and what progress has been made?
5. **The Challenge and Desired Performance:** Discuss the big or strategic challenge of the organization, and suggest next target conditions or performance. First ask the client what he or she feels would be the next appropriate targets.
6. **Feedback:** Ask if he or she has any concerns about his or her role as a team leader.
7. **Problem-solving:** Shared problem-solving in regard to the performance and behavior of the team.
8. **Contracting:** What can I as a coach do to be helpful; and, what do you as a team leader agree to do in the future. Each meeting should

include an agreement on specific tasks and dates. This creates accountability.

CHAPTER 5

THE LEAN COACHING CYCLE

The process of coaching that follows is the result about forty years of trial and error training consultants in my own firm, internal Lean Coaches within my clients' organizations, and attempting to integrate the best of the continual flow of management methods and experience. It is an effort to present the integration of best coaching practices in a simple, practical and easy to follow sequence.

Coaching or consulting is a dynamic, inter-active process. It is non-linear. In other words, you cannot say that there are seven steps, and step three always follows step two. While there is a logical sequence of activities, a skilled coach will be continually thinking about what step makes the most sense given the circumstances with a particular client at a particular time.

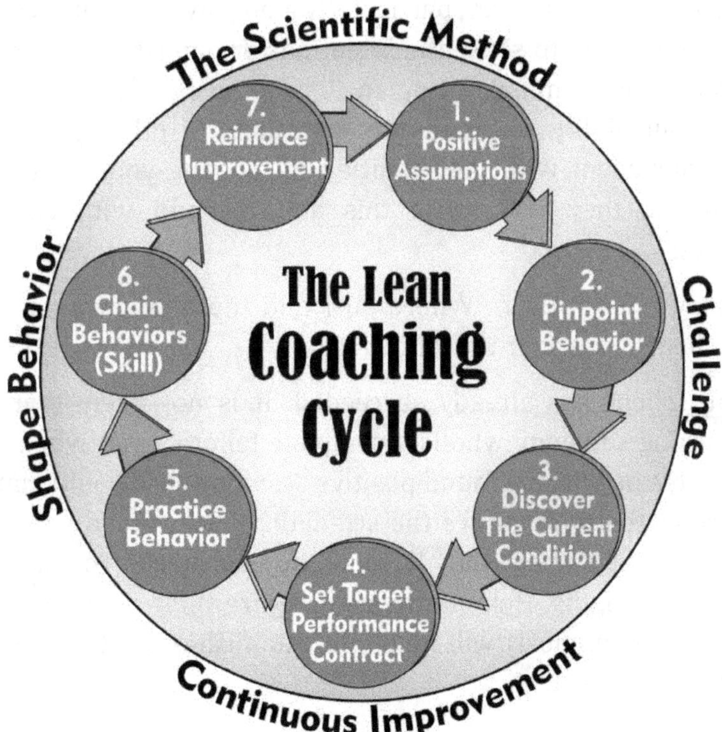

Good coaching is about good judgement and empathy, more than about rigidly following any model.

Here are steps that are typical in a successful lean coaching process:

1. HOLD POSITIVE ASSUMPTIONS:

Some people see the faults in everyone they meet. They have radar that scans the environment for everything that is going wrong, and everything that may go wrong in the future. These unfortunate souls will never make greater coaches. A great coach sees the positive, the good, the opportunity in everyone. Every person you may coach has a current condition and a potential future condition. Your job is to help that individual move from the current to the future, and a positive assumption about the individual and their potential is a necessary condition for success.

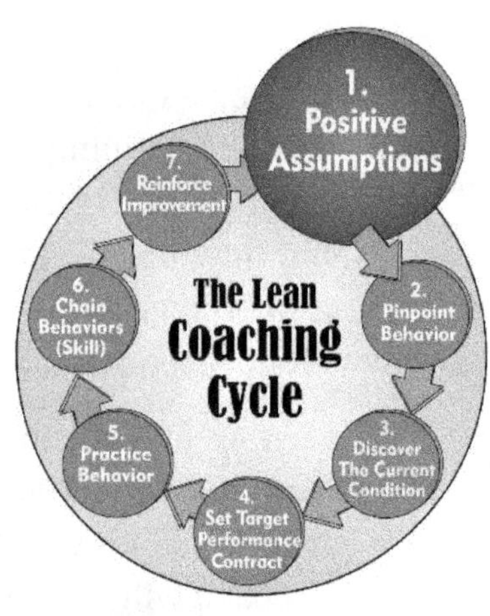

If you are an animal lover, particularly a dog lover, you know that dogs have an innate ability to sense the intentions or danger from approaching people and other animals. Human beings also have an emotional intelligence, an ability to sense the intentions of other people. If you approach your client with the intention of meeting your needs and not meeting theirs, they will sense this and respond with caution and defensiveness.

You may ask yourself, "Where do I find these positive assumptions about my client?" Consider the following:

A. Your client has already succeeded. It is not likely that you are coaching someone who is a complete failure. Even when coaching inmates in prison, I found positive assumptions I could make about each of them. What are the strengths that enabled your client to achieve the success they have already achieved? You can build on those strengths. Helping them recognize their own strengths (we forget sometimes!) will help you establish a positive relationship with your client.

B. Everyone is doing the best they can at the time. Everyone needs to improve. Based on your clients understanding of the system she finds herself in, she is most likely making rational choices. Your job is to help her understand those choices, and consider other choices that may be more in her own best interest.

C. Everyone has something to teach us. As you start a coaching relationship, consider that you may learn as much from your client as they may learn from you. I am forever grateful to my prison inmates for what I was able to learn from them. I have learned great lessons from everyone of my past clients. If you accept that you may learn from your client, the relationship will be more one of mutual learning, and that is always more comfortable for your client.

D. You are not only a coach, but also a model. How you think and how you feel will serve as a model to your client, even though they may not be aware of the modeling effect. If you model optimism and positive emotions, your client is likely to pass those same emotions on to their team and associates.

Groucho Marx said that *"The key to success in life is absolute sincerity and honesty. If you can fake that, you've got it made!"* It's a funny line, but when it comes to coaching, you cannot fake it. When you are preparing for a meeting with someone you are coaching, meditate on your own intentions and say a little prayer, that you will be able to make a positive contribution to this person's life, this day. If you are sincere about being helpful to them, they will sense this, and they will be open to your coaching. If not, it will be much harder to succeed.

When you are planning a coaching relationship or a coaching session, ask yourself the following questions:

- What are my client's strengths that have led to past success? How can I build on those strengths?
- What is my client hoping to achieve? What is his/her best outcome and how can I help them achieve it?
- Compared to how they are performing and the results they are achieving today, what is their potential performance and what obstacles are in their way?

- What fears may they have, and how can I help to alleviate those fears?
- How can I demonstrate my belief in their good intentions, and their ability to improve their performance?
- Plan to listen to their needs or concern with sincere empathy, but without being distracted from the task of achieving some forward progress, some commitment to action.

2. PINPOINT BEHAVIOR:

Every time you hear someone say, "Well, she just has a bad attitude," respond by asking, "Yes, but what is she doing that causes you to feel that she has a bad attitude and how often does she do that?"

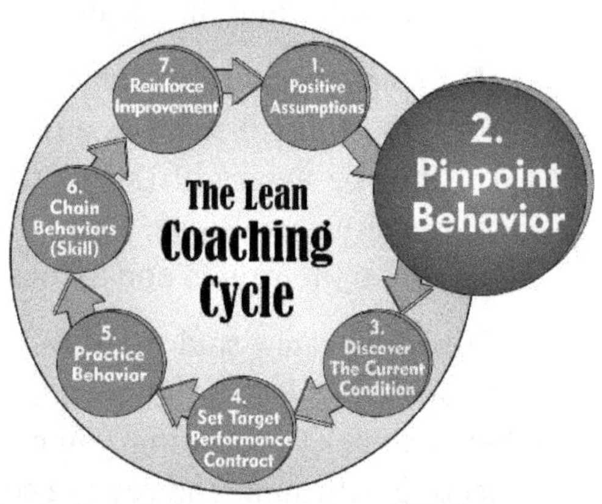

Our culture has made assigning labels a norm, labels such as lazy, ambitious, or unmotivated. These labels are someone's interpretation of someone else's behavior. They are not factual and they have low reliability. They describe something you think is going on inside someone else's head. You cannot see or measure "unmotivated." What you may be seeing is that they walk slowly, or complete X number of tasks when someone else is completing 2X number of tasks.

A pinpointed behavior is a description of exactly what is being observed, which is necessarily outside the person, not inside the person. It is behavior that two or three observers may observe and describe in the same way. This is called *inter-observer reliability*. In other words, if I said, "Jane arrived to work after 8am three out of five days last week," it is likely that three observers would observe the same performance and agree on the same description. But if I said, "Jane doesn't seem to care about her work," it is unlikely that three people would observe her and describe the same thing.

A more important question is: which description will provide helpful feedback to Jane? Will it be helpful to say, "Jane, you don't seem to care about your work?" Or will it be more helpful to describe the pinpointed behavior that is causing you to feel that she doesn't care about her work? Clearly, the latter is more helpful feedback. When you say "You don't seem to care…" you are describing how you feel, not the behavior of the other person. The client is not responsible for your feelings; they are responsible for their behavior.

Another example of pinpointed behavior: Let us assume that you are a coach for implementing lean management and teams. You observe a team meeting in which the team leader you are coaching is facilitating the team meeting. You notice that the team leader is looking at the three members of the team who are sitting on the left side of the room, almost all the time during the meeting. She addresses her comments to those members and rarely, if ever, looks at the members on the right side of the room. The three members to whom she seems to be addressing her comments are those who speak up most often, nod their head in approval, and are giving her attention. Those on the right seem disengaged.

What feedback would you give to this coach? Of course, you could say, "You don't seem to care about half the members of the team." She would probably reply by saying, "What are you talking about, of course I care about them." It would be much more helpful to say, "I noticed that most of your inter-action and eye contact was with the team members to your left. When I noticed that, I started counting the number of comments made by team members on each side of the room. Eight comments were made from the left, only one from the right side of the room. It might be related to your eye contact. At the next meeting why don't you think about this and deliberately look also at those on the right when you make a comment or ask a question. If they don't participate you might ask them a direct question, such as 'how do you feel about this problem (or whatever the topic is). See if they participate more equally then."

This pinpointed behavior will be much more helpful than suggesting that she "doesn't care" about half of the team members. Trying to look inside someone and tell them how you think they feel very often gets a negative response. It is not factual and is somewhat insulting. But the facts of her eye contact and the number of comments from each side of the room are not an effort to interpret her feelings. This factual, pinpointed feedback is much more likely to result in learning and behavior change.

Pinpointed behaviors are:

a. A behavior or result – a behavior consists of someone's actions while a result is what is left when the behavior is completed.

b. Measurable – the behavior or result can be counted as occurring or existing.

c. Observable – the behavior or result can be seen by an observer.

d. Reliable – two independent observers agree.

e. Active – passes the Dead Man's Test (it is not the absence of, but the presence of behavior).

f. Under the performer's control – performer must have major influence on changing the result.

John Austin of Western Michigan University has given the following examples of poor and good pinpointed behaviors:

- *Poor communication.* This is not a good pinpoint because it would be difficult to measure, and for two independent observers to agree. A better pinpoint would be: *Servers write orders on tickets accurately and give them to the kitchen within 2 minutes of the table ordering.*

- *Employees are in a bad mood.* This is difficult to measure and is not reliable. It also is not a behavior or a result and therefore is not observable. A better pinpoint might be: *Employees smile and say, "Welcome to our store, would you like a cart?" as customers enter the store.*

- *There should be food available on site.* This is not a pinpoint but rather a solution to something such as employees taking long breaks to go get food. The pinpoint should be: *Employees return from breaks on time* and the cause and solution are determined after analysis.

- *Employees steal money from the cash registers and give improper change.* This is also not a pinpoint but rather what the employer assumes is the cause of the problem. The real pinpoint is: *Amount of money in employees' cash registers matches register slip at the end of the night.*

3. Discover the Current Condition:

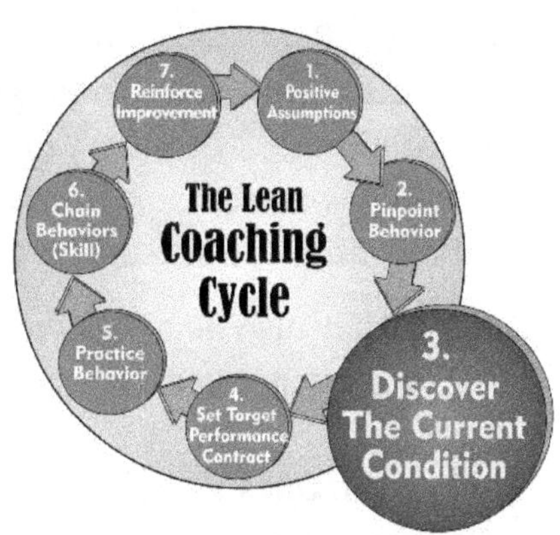

You and your client will want to set challenging targets for improving performance. That target should not be arbitrary. It should be based on a realistic understanding of the current state of performance. That current condition is both performance and behavior. In other words, it may be a rate of production or quality defects; it may also include *who does what to whom, when;* the pinpointed behavior that must change in order to achieve different results.

Where do you begin looking to understand the current condition or current performance?

What is the Current Performance Reality?

Your client is likely to be both an individual manager and his or her team. They have responsibility for performance. Before you can recommend a target condition you must understand their baseline performance.

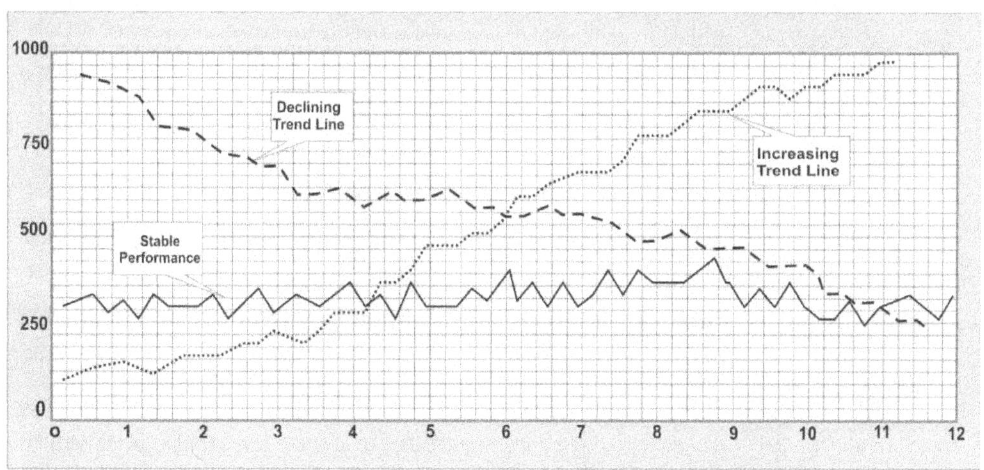

It will set a good model for the manager and for the team if you either study, or create graphs of their baseline performance for four to five key measures of their team's performance. What are the trends in the data? It makes a huge difference if they are going up, down or are stable. Imagine that this graph, and its trend lines, represented three different key variables for your client. Which one or two do you think it would be desirable to focus on? Assuming higher numbers are good, certainly you would target the declining one, and probably the stable baseline as well. Why not the increasing trend line? If performance is already increasing it will be wise to let it continue to run upward.

It may also be helpful to examine the variation in performance. Excess variation represents a cost that can be reduced. If you have a graph of performance you might sit with your client and discuss the pattern of variation. Does she understand why variation occurs and when it occurs? Does she or her team understand the difference between common causes of variation (within the nature of the system), and special causes (errors or defects)? This understanding may present a gap between the current condition and a desired future condition.

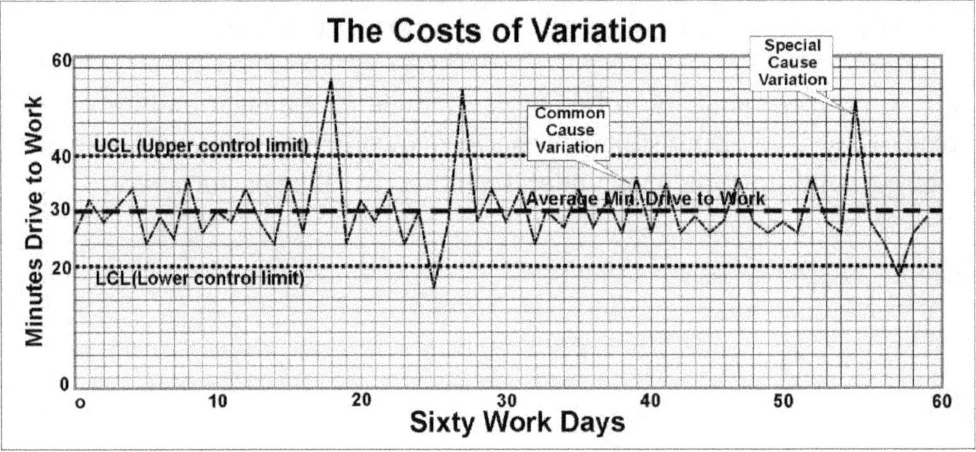

It will be helpful to sit with your client and together discuss the following chart. Your client may have this information, or they may not. A team leader should have knowledge of the key performance variables for each team and should have quick access to current and desired levels. If he or she does not have this information, this lack of knowledge represents a gap between current and desired performance. Then ask the client what specific behavior they might change to improve the key results.

Summary of Current and Desired Condition		
Key Financial Measures	**Current Performance**	**Desired Performance**
Key Customer Satisfaction Measures	**Current Performance**	**Desired Performance**
Key Process Measures (Cycle time, etc.)	**Current Performance**	**Desired Performance**
Key Learning and Development Measures	**Current Performance**	**Desired Performance**

What is on the "Landscape" that will influence your client's work?

All organizations operate on a larger landscape that defines their field of action and influences on their behavior. The landscape is beyond their control. It is the set of forces to which they must adapt and respond. By understanding these influences, you can help your client define the actions that will lead to success.

All living organisms survive by adapting to their environment. All systems that survive are *open-systems,* which simply means that they are open to influence from their environment. The strategic house of every corporation sits on a landscape and that landscape is constantly changing. Modern organizations have no choice but to change, to adapt themselves in response to the changing landscape.

Too often, lean implementations are too slow to address significant issues of adaptation to customer preferences. Many lean consultants assume that using the PDCA cycle on the factory floor is the answer to becoming lean. But, often they are working on processes that should be eliminated entirely or need to be restructured, re-organized, or changed in large and rapid ways.

Lean is very often understood in terms of problem-solving. However, companies and people do not succeed simply by solving problems. They succeed by recognizing challenges, threats and opportunities, that present possibilities of growth. A new technology may not be a problem today; but, it will be when your competitors adopt that technology and you are losing customers as a result. If you recognized the challenge presented by a new technology you might be the one gaining customers at the expense of your competitors.

In the ideal system adaptation would be instantaneous. The moment a new healthcare technology or treatment was developed it would be instantaneously adopted by every healthcare provider. But, of course that doesn't happen. We suffer from the law of *inertia* (*a property of matter by which it remains at rest or in uniform motion in the same straight line unless acted upon by some external force*). The law of inertia applies to human behavior just as it does to physical objects. We tend to stay in our current place or state because it requires less energy than change. The path of least resistance is the path that we are on, even if that path ignores external realities and leads to a cliff.

One function of a coach is to help the client understand the world around him and the opportunities for adaptation to the landscape.

***The Law of Adaptation*:**

Organizations and people progress to the degree that they are capable of sensing shifts on the landscape (economic changes, technology changes, regulatory or political shifts, and changes in social or customer preferences) and then capable of developing those capabilities that will satisfy the market on the future landscape.

Corollaries to the Law of Adaptation:

1. *It is natural for organizations (or people) to remain on their current path and this inevitably leads to wasted energy and market dissatisfaction.*
2. *The speed of changes on the landscape (technology, etc.) defines the necessary capacity to transform the internal capabilities of the organization or for individuals to change their behavior.*
3. *Transformation toward future capabilities requires transformational leadership, the impulse to foresee external changes and to drive internal adaptation by overcoming inertia.*

There are at least eight elements on the landscape that may affect your organization. How do each of these create threats or opportunities for your organization? The following are quick and simple examples.

1. CUSTOMERS:

Customers are the most important part of the landscape for any business. Customer expectations and preferences change daily and they almost always change in the direction of tighter demands, lower cost and more responsive supply delivery. Listening, sensing, and adapting to the needs of customers is one of the most important capabilities for any business.

2. Economic Trends:

For about ten years I consulted with several major oil companies. During that time, they were constantly engaged in scenario planning, attempting to predict the future price of crude oil. The price of crude determines the economic viability of exploration and production activity. In order to justify the costs of exploratory drilling, and then production at a deep-water site in the Gulf of Mexico, oil prices must be above a certain level. Whether to build additional refinery capacity, hire explorationists, invest in property leases, or further exploit existing wells, all is determined by the expected future price of crude oil. The need for internal strategic capabilities (the number of explorationists employed, for example) will determine the ability to meet strategic goals. Every industry has similar relationships with economic activity. Both internal and external strategy (market and financial) are dependent on these economic trends.

3. Political Changes:

Health care has been a subject of political debate for many years. The role the government will play, and the costs and requirements associated with any revision of our health care system are impacting the behavior of every health care provider. This political debate not only affects every company in the health care industry, but every company that currently buys, or may in the future buy, health insurance for its employees. While this will have a huge impact on business in the United States, it is only one of hundreds of ways that political decisions will impact corporations. Sensing and responding intelligently to changes in law is critical to the strategy of every company.

4. Competition:

Innovations may come from within your organization, or they may come from competitors. Successful competition is often the result of carefully watching the behavior of competitors, and adopting competitive strategies. It is often not the first to market who succeeds, but a following competitor who can see where the market is going and which features of a product are most important to customers. Carefully watching the behavior of competitors is essential in business, just as it is in sports.

5. Natural Resources:

Natural resources and the environment may or may not be an influence on your business. However, if you are in the energy, agricultural, housing or many other businesses, the availability of natural resources, their costs, and changes in the environment may be an influence on the direction of your business.

6. Suppliers:

Lean organizations do not operate within one house. They operate in a long series of houses, each adapting to the needs of the other. When Japanese manufacturers moved operations to the United States, one of their greatest concerns was the ability to establish a supplier community that could provide the high quality, just-in-time input required for their operations. They have invested a great deal of resources training and consulting with these suppliers. This attention to the operations of suppliers, many of whom also supplied GM, Ford and Chrysler, had a profound impact on the landscape of the entire industry.

7. Social Trends:

Are you marketing to Latinos? Is your workplace friendly to working mothers? Social trends affect both internal and external relationships. A lack of sensitivity to social changes can lead to big trouble, and the loss of social capital. One of the largest law firms in Atlanta a few years ago had an employee outing at Lake Lanier. As part of the "fun" to welcome new associates they encouraged all the new woman associates to engage in a wet t-shirt contest. This is a law firm that litigates sexual harassment and every other possible offense. What were they thinking! Of course one of their own associates sued them. It is easy to become conditioned to the habits of the old culture and be blinded to social trends... even when your brain should know otherwise.

8. Technology Developments:

It is a rare company that is not required to adapt to changes in technology, changes that will be adopted by competitors and will become expected by customers. Whether it is robots in a factory, financial management software, or new software for decision-making or knowledge management, virtually every company lives on a landscape of competitive technologies.

How Are We Adapting to Our External Landscape?		
FORCES ON THE EXTERNAL LANDSCAPE	HOW HAVE WE ADAPTED AND HAS THAT BEEN SUCCESSFUL?	HOW MUST WE ADAPT IN THE FUTURE?
Customers		
Economic Trends		
Political Changes		
Competitors		
Natural Resources		
Suppliers		
Social Trends		
Technology		

4. Contracting for A Target Performance

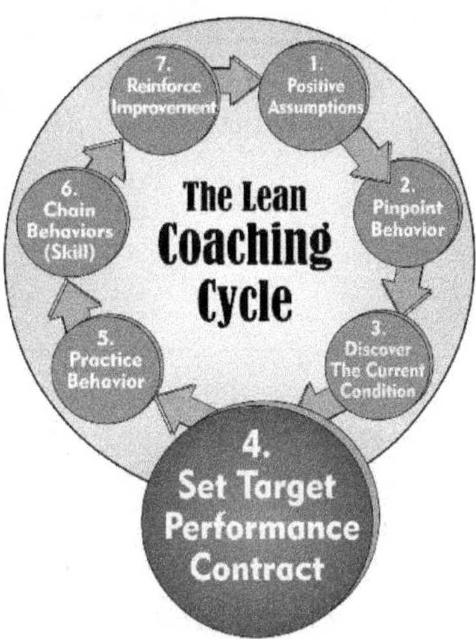

One way to understand the contribution of a coach is to see her as helping the client focus on the right things. The coach can help her client to make commitments to action, and hold them accountable as they move toward their desired future performance. Whether they are written down or simply verbal, the commitments between a coach and a client may be viewed as a contract.

When deciding on target performance the coach should help the client consider the larger challenge presented by senior managers. An individual manager may be satisfied with current performance, however, the strategy of the organization may require achieving lower costs, higher productivity or quality. This is the challenge that the individual client should accept. Deciding exactly how to respond to that challenge is the work of the coach and client.

The coach may propose a course of action or may ask the client to suggest a course of action. There are many ways that a proposed course of action can be developed. It is more important how a course of action is arrived at than exactly what it is. If you are developing a culture of continuous improvement you want the client, both her as a team leader, and her team, to take ownership for their own performance. Therefore, it is not wise for the coach to appear to be the expert instructing the client as to the next target performance. Rather, it is wise to ask the client to suggest future targets, although the coach should feel free to make suggestions.

You should develop a proposed course of action with the client, not for the client. It is important that the course of action is the result of genuine consultation. Here are some questions to ask yourself and your client as you develop a proposed course of action:

Questions to Consider in Developing a Proposed Course of Action	
Is the goal or purpose clear to the client?	
Have we agreed on the measures that will indicate success?	
Do we agree on who will participate in our course of action and how they will participate?	
Does the client understand her role in making this plan successful?	
Have I established a trusting, frank and honest relationship with this client?	
Have we agreed on a timeline?	
Have we agreed, or do we have a common understanding of funding?	
Have we agreed on communications? Who will communicate what to whom?	

CONTRACTING WITH THE CLIENT:

A contract is an agreement to perform in a desired way. Behavior contracts have long been used in schools and homes to build desired performance on the part of children. They are even used in the discipline of self-management. But they are just as helpful when coaching a leader in the workplace.

When you are having the discussions outlined in the coaching cycle you should be listening for statements such as "OK, I guess I need to attend all of the team's meetings" or other statements of intended and desired behavior. Of course, you will nod your head and verbally agree with these intentions if you feel they are what is needed. It will also be desirable for you to write down the agreed upon behavior, and formalize this in a contract, either written or verbal. Making the desired behavior on the part of the team leader explicit, rather than assumed or implied, greatly increases the likelihood that the team leader will follow through on that behavior.

The "Performance Contract" on the following page may be helpful to formalize agreement on future behavior on the part of both the leader and the coach. You are likely most interested in the team leader agreeing to perform differently in the future, and less interested in how the team leader may wish you to perform differently. However, by presenting the contract as a mutual agreement, you will find the team leader to be much more willing to participating.

You may find it helpful to practice a conversation with a fellow coach, acting as a team leader, to prepare yourself for your meeting.

Coach – Team Leader **Performance Contract**		
The Leader Agrees to Do the Following	**When Will this Be Done?**	**Date and Status**
The Coach Agrees to Do the Following	**When Will this Be Done?**	**Date and Status**

5. Practice the Behavior - Action-Learning

Continuous improvement should follow a cycle of action-learning. We are attempting to build new skills and habits. Skills or habits only develop as a result of repeated practice, feedback and more practice.

The best methods and the best of intentions can easily fail unless we take into account how adults learn in our organizations. During World War II a process that has become known as *Training Within Industry* (TWI) and its component *Job Instruction* (JI) was developed in the United States. It was later adopted by Toyota as it developed its system of production. For management development Toyota and other Japanese companies added the role of the *sensei* or coach. These methods are effective because they are consistent with *action-learning* that is based on the reality of how adults learn.

Malcom Knowles who pioneered the field of adult learning identified the following principles as critical to adult learning:

- Adults are autonomous and self-directed. They need to be free to direct themselves. Their teachers must actively involve adult participants in the learning process and serve as facilitators for them. They must show participants how the learning experience will help them reach their goals.
- Adults have accumulated a foundation of life experiences and knowledge that may include work-related activities, family responsibilities and previous education. They need to connect learning to this knowledge/experience base.
- Adults are goal-oriented. Instructors must show participants how learning will help them attain their goals.
- Adults are relevancy-oriented. They must see a reason for learning something. Learning has to be applicable to their work or other responsibilities to be of value to them.

- Adults are practical, focusing on the aspects of a lesson most useful to them in their work. They may not be interested in knowledge for its own sake. Instructors must tell participants explicitly how the lesson will be useful to them on the job.
- As do all learners, adults need to be shown respect. Instructors must acknowledge the wealth of experiences that adult participants bring to the classroom. These adults should be treated as equals in experience and knowledge, and allowed to voice their opinions freely.

Another way of saying this is simply to say that adults aren't good at sitting at a desk and obediently following instructions and learning theories or abstractions. Learning has to make a difference to them, and they have to put it into action. I think the same could be said for children.

Imagine learning to play a musical instrument. How much knowledge of the keyboard or fret board is useful without then putting your hands on the instrument and practicing? The answer is very little. The important learning comes from playing the instrument, hearing the sounds, trying out different positions and chords and experiencing their difference. At one point I had the idea that I would learn to play the banjo, and I bought a lesson book by Pete Seeger. When he was asked how often you should practice his answer was "Never. Just play!" What he understood was that the learning will come from the joy of playing, not from doing exercises or turning the experience into a painful task.

Learning any new skill is much the same way. Teams need to practice problem-solving and experiment. It is OK to fail as long as every effort is recognized as a learning experience.

Practicing, evaluating, improving becomes a way of life. A Fast Company article (6/2/2009) on Toyota's Georgetown, KY plant described the reflection of one worker in the plant: *"Artrip has been at Georgetown for 19 years. The way he does his work is so compelling it has become part of his personal life. 'When I'm mowing the grass, I'm thinking about the best way to do it. I'm trying different turns to see if I can do it faster,' he says."* This is a clear sign that continuous improvement has become ingrained in the culture through repeated practice.

6. Build the Skill - Chain the Behaviors

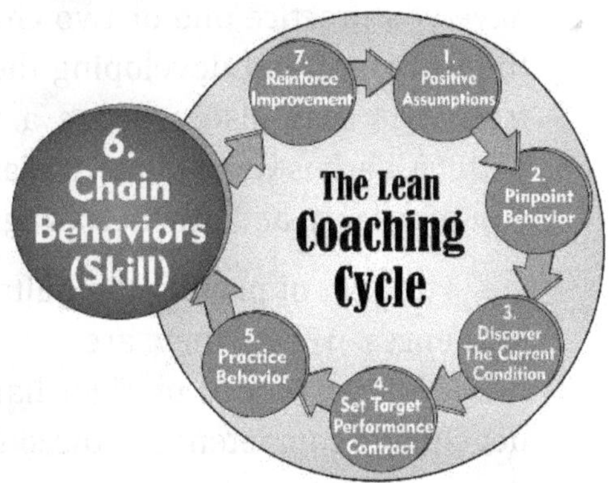

If you are teaching a complex skill, such as facilitating a team meeting, you will break that skill down into its component behaviors. For example, the following are some specific behaviors that are components of the team facilitation skills:

- Starting the meeting on time.
- Reviewing the agenda.
- Reviewing action items from prior meetings.
- Review performance data.
- Asking members for their analysis of the data.
- Asking for the team to identify problems or opportunities for improvement based on the data.
- Leading the team in the PDSA problem-solving cycle.
- Identifying experiments and action steps.

When you look at any one of these pinpointed behaviors, you would not call them a skill on their own. When they are put together in a behavioral chain, and that chain is performed fluently, we may call that a skill. Leading a meeting or leading problem-solving is a skill comprised of many pinpointed behaviors.

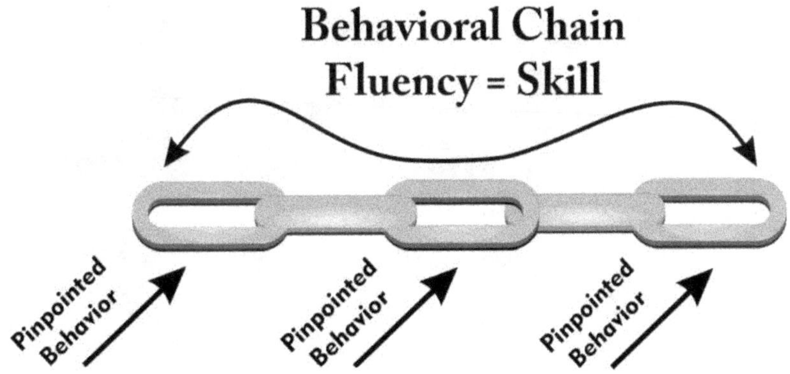

It is easy to understand achieving fluency if you have learned to play a musical instrument. When learning to play the guitar the instructor will have you practice one or two chords, learning to position your fingers on the fretboard and developing the strength to hold the strings against the frets. You may also practice a right hand strumming or finger picking pattern. Each is very simple. But as you acquire competence in one behavior, you then learn and practice a slightly more difficult behavior.

The skill of playing the guitar is the result of many separate learning sequences. When they are practiced in a chain, with fluid movement between each chord or right hand pattern, then we can say that we are developing competence in the skill.

Remember the principle of behavior shaping. At first you practice very simple behaviors, then gradually more difficult. But the behavior must be reinforced if it is to become habit. When you look at the list of behaviors on the previous page, imagine yourself observing a team meeting. Many things may not go well. But the team leader has probably succeeded in some of these behaviors. It is important that the coach is noticing these and giving the team leader positive feedback after the meeting. Then you can also point to one or two behaviors that could be improved at the next meeting.

Look at the team meeting observation checklist and feedback form in the third part of this book. The purpose of this is to help you structure your observations so that you are not only noticing what needs improvement, but you are also noticing what is being accomplished.

7. Reflection and Reinforcement:

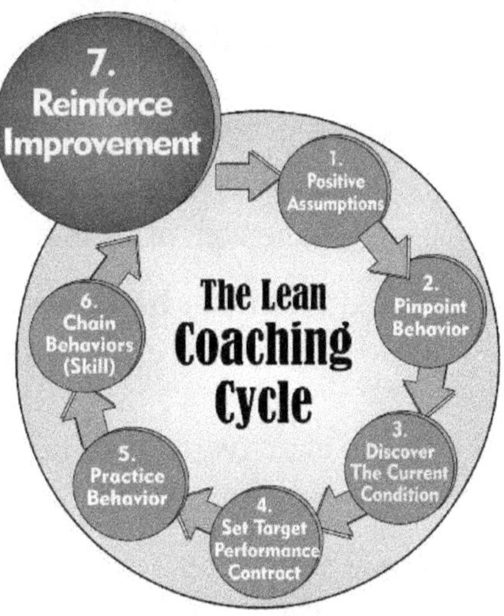

In order to be effective in shaping the behavior of both teams and team leaders the coach must reinforce desired behavior or performance. If the coach comes to be seen only as a source of criticism, the client will avoid the coach and reject his or her advice.

In preparation for each meeting, consider what you have observed that is positive. Any effort on the part of the client or the team is worthy of positive comment by the coach. Remember the four-to-one principle: the highest performance is achieved by a preponderance of positive reinforcement rather than negative remarks.

Think about your next meeting with your client. What action has he or she taken that is positive? What do you plan to say about these desired behaviors?

When you meet with a team leader your purpose should not be to correct every fault of either the team or its leader. Rather, it should be to make progress, to move one step closer to becoming a high performing team and a successful leader of that team. It is never a good idea to dump too much on the team leader. Your job is to gradually shape the behavior of the team and its leader, and this is best done in small doses.

Assessing the progress of the team and giving the leader feedback is best done as a casual conversation, rather than a formal assessment and feedback. It is best that each of your meetings with the team leader include this conversation. Your assessment and feedback conversation might include the following components:

- **Self-assessment:** Ask the team leader how he feels the team is performing. There is a good chance that the team leader will see the same positives and negatives that you are seeing. In this case it is desirable that the assessment come from the team leader. You can then offer your own clarification and suggest steps that can be taken to move forward.

- **What is going well?** No matter how many problems a team or team leader may be having, there is always something that has been done right. It is important that you demonstrate that you are not "negative" in general. If the team leader perceives you as someone who just sees the negative side of things, this will discredit your feedback. Be sure to point out something that the team leader has done well or, something that the team has done well.
- **What can be improved?** What would you like for the team leader to do differently (more or less of) in the future? Rather than saying "You aren't doing this, or you did a bad job of..." It will be more effective to say "In the future it will be helpful if you..." and then state the desired behavior in positive terms.
- **What can I, as a coach, do to be more helpful?** It will be very useful for you as a coach to ask for advice and feedback from the team leader. This makes the feedback session a two way, adult-to-adult process, rather than simply a one way, or "parent-child" relationship. By asking the team leader how you can be more helpful, you may find that the team leader is then more willing to participate in improvement himself.

Positive Reinforcement and the 4 to 1 Rule

Toyota practices Four-to-One.[7] What does it mean and where does it come from?

In 1973 I joined Aubrey Daniels and Fran Tarkenton in Atlanta where they had just started Behavioral Systems, Inc. The company was focused on spreading the use of positive reinforcement in industry. Around that time a behavioral psychologist named Dr. Ogden Lindsley did research in classrooms to determine what ratio of positive to negative comments by teachers resulted in the highest rate of learning by students. The answer: 3.57 to 1. Since we expected that no one would remember 3.57 to 1, we rounded it off to 4 to 1. Our training and consultants promoted the 4 to 1 principle.

For several years we worked in southern textile mills teaching supervisors to *Catch Someone Doing Something Good Today,* and we had

[7] Liker, Jeffrey K. and Hoseus, Michael. Toyota Culture. New York, McGraw-Hill, 2008, p. 403.

them record their own interactions with employees. How many of those interactions were positive and how many were negative? How many were recognizing good behavior and how many were criticizing bad behavior? Initially, most supervisors found that they were more likely to be 1 to 4, rather than 4 to 1, in other words, four times more negative than positive.

Every parent should know that punishing bad behavior may suppress that behavior, but if you don't reward the opposite good behavior the child is likely to misbehave in another way. You must define the desired alternative behavior, and reward that behavior. We do what pays off in a positive way. You get what you reward! If you want good performance you must positively reinforce good behavior.

Adam Grant, who teaches organizational behavior at the Wharton Business School, has conducted research that demonstrates how employees, even in relatively mundane jobs, may be motivated by altruism – the desire to do good for others:

> *"Over the years, Grant has followed up that study with other experiments testing his theories about pro-social motivation — the desire to help others, independent of easily foreseeable payback. In one study, Grant put up two different signs at hand-washing stations in a hospital. One reminded doctors and nurses, "Hand hygiene prevents you from catching diseases"; another read, "Hand hygiene prevents patients from catching diseases." Grant measured the amount of soap used at each station. Doctors and nurses at the station where the sign referred to their patients used 45 percent more soap or hand sanitizer.*
>
> *"These studies, two of Grant's best known, focus on typically worthy beneficiaries: needy students and vulnerable patients. But some of his other research makes the case that pro-social behavior is as applicable in corporate America as it is in a hospital or a university. "Think of it this way," he said. "In corporate America, people do sometimes feel that the work they do isn't meaningful. And contributing to co-workers can be a substitute for that."*[8]

Adam Grant's experiments demonstrate that workers will be motivated to do well by their fellow workers. But that shouldn't be news to us. Approval by our team members, and being of service to our team members is often more important than recognition from above. Everyone who has

---

[8] New York Times Magazine, March 31, 2013. *Is Giving the Secret to Getting Ahead?*

played on a sports team, at any level, has experienced the power of peer approval.

THE POWER OF FEEDBACK

Few influences have been the subject of as many research projects as the effect of feedback on human performance. Let's make it simple: feedback that is *immediate, specific* and *positive* has the most influence on behavior. There are few things that a leader or manager does that have more influence on human performance. As a coach, you want to provide effective feedback to your clients; and, you want help them provide effective feedback to their team members.

The guidelines for giving and receiving feedback on the following page are good rules to follow. You may also find behavior observation sheet that follows to be helpful in identifying feedback for your team leader. When considering what feedback to give to your client, ask yourself the following questions:

- **Self-Assessment:** What question(s) might you ask to elicit a self-assessment on the part of your client?
- **What is going well?** What will you share with your team leader in the form of positive observations?
- **What can be improved?** What feedback will you give to your team leader to encourage positive behavior that will improve his or her leadership of the team?
- **What can I, as a coach, do to be more helpful?** What is the exact question or questions that you will ask the team leader to elicit feedback from him to you?

GUIDELINES FOR GIVING FEEDBACK

The following guidelines may be helpful when considering how to give your team leader feedback.

a. Be sure that your intention is to be helpful to the other person or team.

b. Think it through. Be clear about what you want to say. Even if you are not sure about the reasons why you feel the way you do, you can share that uncertainty.

c. Emphasize the positive. You care about this person or group and you want to help them improve. Tell them why you care.

d. Be specific -- Avoid general comments or exaggerations. Don't say "You always..." This will cause the other person to be defensive. Be specific about what and when the person or group does something.

e. Focus on pinpointed behavior rather than the person. The person is good and worthy, but the behavior is what needs to be improved, and it is also what the person can change.

f. Own the feedback -- Use 'I' statements to indicate that this is how "I feel and others may not experience the same thing."

g. Your manner and the feelings you express are important. Be direct, but be kind and helpful. Be sincere.

Guidelines for Receiving Feedback

We can all benefit from feedback... if we listen well and seek to understand in a way that will promote our own learning and development. Here are some guidelines for receiving feedback from others:

a. Understand that the person giving you feedback is attempting to be helpful. Try to receive the feedback as a gift given to you by this person who wishes to help you succeed.

b. Listen for actionable feedback. Ask yourself "What can I do differently in the future based on this feedback?" Do not focus on the person giving you the feedback or how you feel about that individual.

c. Ask for clarification. Ask when or under what circumstances you do something. Ask for examples that can clarify the situation or behavior. Ask the other person what you might do as an alternative in that situation. Seek to understand.

d. Engage in problem-solving. Think together about the problem.

e. Summarize what you have heard. Reflect back to the person giving you feedback your understanding of what you have heard.

f. Take responsibility for your behavior and demonstrate a willingness to modify your own behavior.

g. Remember that this feedback is not an evaluation of how good a person you are, but how your behavior is perceived by others at certain times.

Behavior Observations

Use the following to record observations of behavior in preparation for giving feedback to a team leader. Remember to pinpoint behavior in a way that two persons will see the same thing. Do not record “attitudes” or your own feelings.

Behavior Observation Sheet		
Helpful Behaviors	**Effects on You and the Team**	**Possible Alternatives**
Unhelpful Behaviors	**Effects on You and the Team**	**Possible Alternatives**

Gaining the Help of Others:

Sometimes, all of the above steps do not lead to success in shaping the behavior of your client. Sometimes you will need to seek the help of the manager at the next level above.

You need to think carefully about this. Clearly, this may damage your relationship with the client if he or she feels you have not given them the opportunity to do the right thing first. Ask yourself the following questions before considering this step:

- Have I given the client direct and clear feedback on his lack of performance?
- Have I gone through each of the steps outlined above in order to shape his behavior?
- Has the client had sufficient time to improve his performance?
- Have I considered other time pressures and priorities that may have prevented the client from following through on the desired performance?
- Before going to the next step, have I expressed my own frustration to the client?

If you have done these things and still not succeeded in gaining support and change on the part of the client, it is then time for you to share your concerns with the leader at the next level above. How you do this is important.

Ask the leader above for help. Rather than condemning the client, tell the next level manager that "I don't feel like I am getting through to him. I have tried everything I know to do, but he is still not attending the meetings of his team (or state the deficiency clearly). Can you help me out and observe the team meetings yourself and give (name of client) your own observation and recommendation?"

Ultimately, the manager above is responsible for the performance of each of the team leaders below. But rather than pointing out their responsibility, which they should recognize, it will be more effective for you to ask for their help. In preparation for this conversation you should think clearly and carefully about what you will say and ask of the manager.

a. What is the pinpointed behavior that you would like the client to engage in?

b. What have you already done to elicit this behavior?

c. What are the specifics of the client's current behavior that you find unacceptable?

d. What exactly would you like the manager to do?

IMPROVE - CONTINUOUSLY

No one is expected to know the one right way for all times. Everyone is expected to engage in continuous improvement. As was said earlier, it is important that you be a model of the behavior you are trying to create within the organization.

The phrase *"I have learned something from this"*, or *"I can do that better next time"* are phrases that are not a sign of failure, but a sign of learning and processing feedback. They are a sign of strength and not weakness. You should make statements like this with pride, pride that you are also engaged in learning and improvement.

Exactly how are you going to improve your own skills as a coach? Here are some suggestions:

- First, be a member of a team of coaches who work together to process their own work, identify things that are both working and not working. It is much easier to learn and improve as part of a team, rather than alone. Remember that other coaches will be struggling with the same issues with which you are struggling.
- Second, ask your client for feedback. It will set a good model for you to ask them for feedback on how a training session went or on how you are coaching them.
- Third, be sure to individualize and be creative with each coaching session. Even after many years of doing this kind of work, it is still necessary to think through every session in terms of what is important for your client.
- Ask for help. Humility is the first virtue that leads to improvement. Arrogance is the greatest enemy of improvement. If you ask your

client or team for help, they will almost always give it. If you ask other coaches for help, they will always give it. When you ask for help everyone wins because it is a learning opportunity for those who provide help.

PART TWO

SKILLS AND PERSPECTIVES THAT WILL BE HELPFUL TO LEAN COACHES

Chapter 6

What is Lean Management, Anyway?

If you are to be a lean coach, you must first know what "it" is. There are many dozens of books on lean or Toyota Production System from which you can gain a great deal of understanding. Jeff Liker's books are certainly among the best. However, I thought it would be helpful to share a simple and direct definition that you may use with your clients.

If someone tells you that "lean management is this" and not something else, if someone puts it in a box and ties a bow around it and presents it in a neat package with four walls around it, then that someone knows not of what they speak. Why? Because it is in motion and not a framed picture hanging on the wall. It is a melody, a rhythm, and not a single note. Lean is a culture and cultures are always complex. In a country the culture is not only how people behave, it is also the system of education, the economy, the justice system and the system of governance. All of these are constantly interacting with one another and impacting human behavior. Organizations are very similar and if we want to change the culture we must be able to think about the complex system.

One way to understand any culture is to recognize that first, there are basic ***principles***; second, there are ***systems and structures*** that are required to support the principles; third, there are defined ***practices***; and finally, there are ***habits***. For example, in Western democracies such as the United States, there are the big ideas of freedom of speech, of press and religion, and the right to vote. But, these principles would be meaningless without supportive systems and structures. For example, the Constitution, legislative, executive and judicial branches of government are structures; and, the system of elections support the principles. Then the government passes laws which define practices. Finally, there must be the habits of free expression and voting. There are parallels within the culture of every organization.

How does this definition of culture translate to the world of lean? First, there are the big ***principles*** of lean – continuous improvement and respect for people. These are not hollow slogans; they are important ideas upon which everything else is based. The ***systems*** of developing leaders at Toyota supports these principles. The systems of continuous improvement through daily problem solving and the information and decision-making systems are important elements of the culture. The ***structures*** that may create walls between functions, or levels that may separate decision makers from the value-adding work, and the structure of teams, may all support or detract from adherence to stated principles. The ***practices*** of lean include the ability of employees to stop the line by pulling the Andon cord (recently replaced with yellow call buttons that stop the line) which is a clear reflection of the principle of respect for people. Standard work and leader standard work are practices that establish standard ways of doing a job which can then be the subject of continuous improvement. Going to the Gemba, the place where the work is done, is an essential practice for managers. And, then there are all the ***habits*** that include the habits of problem-solving, not blaming others, four-to-one, and the simple mental habit of continuously looking at the data and imagining better ways of doing things.

The lean coach will want to consider all of these principles, systems and structures, practices and habits as they seek to build lean culture in their organization.

Lean Principles

Lean management is generally derived from the Toyota Production System as developed by Taiichi Ohno, Shigeo Shingo and others over a forty-year period. It began with efforts to reduce die change time on the stamping press, which then allowed for a reduction of in-process inventory and this became *just-in-time* inventory management. This resulted in the need for less warehouse space, fewer forklifts, unnecessary space, etc. Once the flow of work can be interruption free, free of materials sitting, standing, and redo-loops, waste is eliminated. Lean is the elimination of waste. But, more importantly, lean is continuous improvement in all work processes.

In order to improve the work of the die press and reduce waste, Shingo did not simply give instructions to the workers. He asked the workers to think. He challenged them to innovate and find ways to speed the process by eliminating unnecessary activities. The workers who operated the press and changed dies worked as a team, and together they solved problems and sought improvement. It was the front line workers, who were on-the-spot, and who were truly the world's greatest experts in their work, who experimented, watched the data, and learned from the facts.

This model of improving the work process by those who do the work, by those who are on-the-spot (the *Gemba*), is the essence of lean management. The model of Shingo asking the work team to think, to experiment, and to learn from the data, is the model of lean management. It is management that is humble and not arrogant. It is management that observes, encourages, challenges and learns. It is management that gathers the facts, encourages experimentation, and spreads best practices. It is management that practices what they preach to others.

This model was quickly copied by Honda and other Japanese companies, and has now become the standard of world class manufacturing. And, it has become the standard for management in all types of work settings.

Lean is a moving target because, at its heart, lean is a process of learning and improvement. It cannot be defined as something that is standing still or fixed. It is not simply mimicking what happened at Toyota or anywhere else. And, most importantly, it is not a kaizen event, a project, or something done by a consultant.

It can also be viewed as a philosophy rather than a particular method or technique. If you don't have the philosophy, you don't get it.

Here are some ways of describing lean culture:

- Lean is a culture of continuous improvement practiced by every team and at every level of the organization.
- Lean is the application of the scientific method of experimentation and the study of work processes and systems to find and implement improvements.
- Lean is respect for people. It is respecting the voice of the customer and it is respect for those who do the work, who are "on-the-spot" and are, therefore, the "world's greatest experts" in their work.
- Lean is the elimination of waste in all its forms. It is the ability to distinguish between work that actually adds value to your customers and work that does not. By eliminating waste, you free resources to devote to value-adding activity that serves your customers.
- Lean is a work environment that assures the quality and safety of all work for both customers and staff.
- Lean is a focus on improving the work process and not on blaming people or creating fear.
- Lean is a culture of teamwork, shared responsibility and ownership that cuts through organization walls or silos.
- Lean is a culture that returns the joy to work. Honda speaks of the three joys of buying, selling and making the product. We do our best work when we have joy in our work.
- Lean is flow. Lean is an interruption free process that flows from beginning to end without interruption.

Within lean management are the lessons learned from generations of experimentation in management. The work of Frederick Taylor and Henry Ford are not dismissed, but incorporated and built upon. All of the work in industrial and organizational psychology are incorporated. The work of total Quality leaders such as Dr. Deming, Shewhart and Juran are incorporated. The work of Fred Emery and Eric Trist who founded the school of socio-technical systems is integral to the nature of lean organization. Toyota alone, did not invent good management. Toyota and

Honda simply did a superior job of learning and applying the lessons to which many others contributed.

Your job as a coach is to incorporate these lessons within your own management system, and seek improvement... continuously.

Social and Technical Systems

It is useful to understand that any culture, and lean culture in particular, is a socio-technical system. Different authors and practitioners of lean may place more emphasis on either the social or technical systems. This author addresses the social systems or culture more than the technical side of lean. In practice they are equally important and they are inter-dependent. There are many aspects to the technical side of lean. These include just-in-time material flow, Kanban, Poke-A-Yoke, continuous line flow, etc. The social systems include the training and development of people, the decision processes, teamwork, problem-solving and the systems of motivation. The following is an attempt to illustrate these two sides to lean.

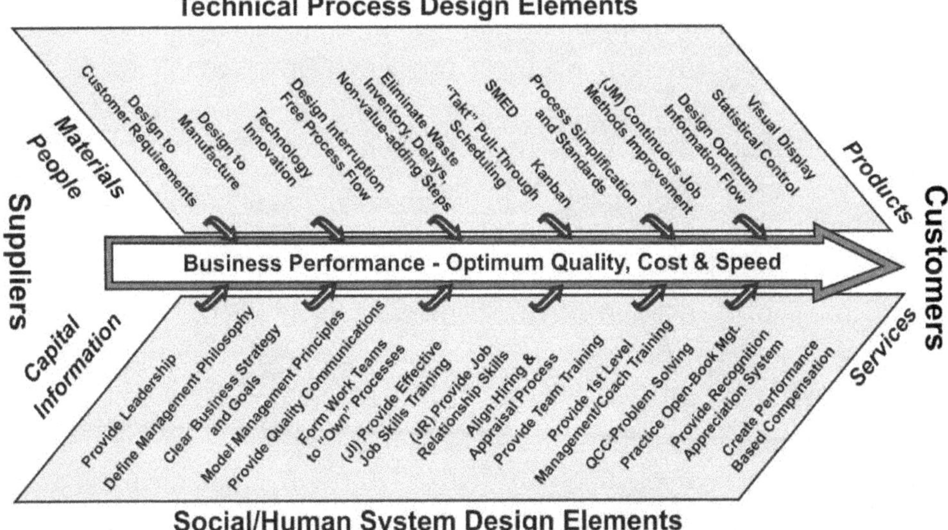

It is useful for the coach to ask himself whether the challenge facing his current organization is more one of technical systems or social systems. There are many paths toward improvement, and no organization can address them all at the same time. Each element of lean requires a different solution and, as a coach, you may be expert in some of them, but not all of them. The best coaches will know when they need to call on additional expertise to address different issues.

CHAPTER 7

HELPING AND HUMAN RELATIONS SKILLS

Early in my career, almost by accident, I found myself as the single counselor for 350 young inmates at a North Carolina prison. With no training in counseling, I acquired Robert R. Carkhuff's *Helping and Human Relations, Volumes 1 and 2.*[9] I didn't know it at the time, but this work of Carkhuff's became a classic in the field of counseling.

Carkhuff identified seven major skills that a coach (he used the term *helper*) should have to successfully serve a client. It is worth reviewing these characteristics and ask yourself whether or not you demonstrate these skills.

> *The coach is a person who is living effectively himself or herself and who discloses himself in a genuine and constructive fashion in his response to others. She communicates an accurate empathic understanding and a respect for all of the feelings of the other person and guides discussions with those persons into specific feelings and experiences.*

1. EMPATHY:

The ultimate purpose of the empathic response is to communicate to the client a depth of understanding of her predicament in such a manner that she can expand and clarify her own self-understanding as well as her understanding of others. The guidelines for empathy are:

---

[9] Carkhuff, Robert R. *The Art of Helping*, 9th Edition (current edition). Possibilities Publishing, Amherst, MA, 2009.

The coach concentrates with intensity upon the client's expressions, verbal and non- verbal.

a. *The coach concentrates upon responses that are interchangeable with those of the client.*
b. *The coach formulates his responses in language that is most attuned to the client.*
c. *The coach responds in a feeling tone similar to that communicated by the client.*
d. *The coach is most effective in communicating empathic understanding when he is most responsive.*
e. *The coach moves tentatively toward expanding and clarifying the client's experiences at higher levels.*
f. *The coach concentrates upon what is not being said.*

2. Respect: The communication of respect to the client has several purposes:

- *To establish a relationship based upon trust and confidence in which the client can explore relevant concerns;*
- *To establish a basis on which the client can come to respect herself in areas relevant to her effective functioning;*
- *To establish a modality through which the client can, with appropriate discriminations, come to respect others in areas relevant to his own functioning. The guidelines for the communication of respect are as follows:*

1. *The coach suspends all critical judgments concerning the client.*
2. *The coach communicates to the client in at least minimally warm and modulated tones.*
3. *The coach concentrates upon understanding the client.*
4. *The coach gives the client the opportunity to make himself known in ways that might elicit positive regard from the coach.*

5. *The coach communicates in a genuine and spontaneous manner.*

3. CONCRETENESS:

The communication of concreteness enables the client to deal specifically with all areas of personally relevant concern. Being concrete is much like pinpointing behavior. It is being specific enough so that the client is not left wondering about the meaning of a statement. The guidelines for the communication of concreteness are:

1. *The coach makes concrete his own reflections and interpretations.*
2. *The coach emphasizes the personal relevance of the client's communications.*
3. *The coach asks for specific details and specific instances. The coach relies upon his own experiences as a guideline for determining whether concreteness is appropriate or not.*

4. GENUINENESS AND SELF-DISCLOSURE:

Genuineness provides both the goal of helping and the necessary contextual base within which helping takes place. The dimension of self-disclosure serves a complementary role to genuineness. The guidelines for communication of these dimensions are as follows:

1. *The coach attempts to minimize the effects of his role, professional or otherwise.*
2. *The coach communicates no inauthentic responses while she demonstrates authentic responses.*
3. *The coach increasingly attempts to be as open and free within the helping relationship as is possible.*
4. *The coach can share experiences with the client as fully as possible.*
5. *The coach can learn to make open-ended inquiries into the most difficult areas of his experience.*
6. *The coach relies upon his experiences as the best guideline.*

5. CONFRONTATION:

In order to enable the client to confront herself effectively when appropriate, the coach must confront the client for the following discrepancies in her own behavior: discrepancies between the client's expression of who or what she wishes to be and how she actually experiences herself or how others experience her. The following guidelines may be employed in formulating confrontation responses:

1. *The coach concentrates upon the client's expressions, both verbal and non-verbal.*
2. *The coach concentrates initially upon raising questions concerning discrepant communications from the client.*
3. *The coach focuses grounding the client in factual information.*

6. IMMEDIACY:

With regard to interpretation of the immediacy of the relationship, the key question is, "'what is the client really trying to tell me that he cannot directly tell me?" The guidelines for communication of immediacy are as follows:

1. *The coach concentrates on his own personal experience in the immediate moment*
2. *The coach temporarily disregards for the moment the content of the client's expression.*
3. *The coach periodically sits back and searches the key question of' immediacy.*

NOTES:

1. The following two books are also excellent resources for coaches:

Co-Active Coaching - Changing Business, Transforming Lives: Henry Kimsey-House, et al, 2011, Nicholas Brealey Publishing.

Coaching for Leadership: Marshall Goldsmith and Laurence Lyons, 2006, Pfeiffer.

CHAPTER 8

THE SCIENCE OF POSITIVE INTERACTION

I previously referred to the "four-to-one principle." Simply stated, this says that both learning and motivation on the part of individuals are optimized when the ratio of positive to negative interactions with managers or coaches are close to four positive interactions to one negative. Higher rates of negative interactions reduce learning, increase fear, and increase avoidance behavior, rather than problem-solving and experimentation. As Judith Glaser has reported, positive interactions produce "conversational intelligence" and, negative interactions surely produce the reverse.

NEW SCIENCE AND OLD RESEARCH

The original research for this was conducted by Dr. Ogden Lindsley, the father of *precision learning,* which has a lot in common with lean coaching and job development methods. Lindsley studied the teacher-student interactions and divided them into positive (approving, praising, etc.), neutral, and negative (wrong answer, correcting behavior) and found that the highest rates of learning were achieved when the teacher's behavior was 3.57 to one, positive to negative. For many years I have taken this and rounded it off to 4-to-1, and encouraged managers to consider their interactions with employees or team members in this light. Positive comments increase learning and motivation and this is critical to the leader's job.

Judith E. Glaser recently published an article in the Harvard Business Review Blog titled *"The Neurochemistry of Positive Conversations."* It is worth reading. New research often confirms old research from the perspective of a new science. It seems that neuroscience confirms a bio-chemical effect of positive and negative interactions:

> *"When we face criticism, rejection or fear, when we feel marginalized or minimized, our bodies produce higher levels of cortisol, a hormone that shuts down the thinking center of our brains and activates conflict aversion and protection behaviors. We become more reactive and sensitive. We often perceive even greater judgment and negativity than actually exists. And these effects can last for 26 hours or more, imprinting the interaction on our memories and magnifying the impact it has on our future behavior. Cortisol functions like a sustained-release tablet – the more we ruminate about our fear, the longer the impact.*
>
> *"Positive comments and conversations produce a chemical reaction too. They spur the production of oxytocin, a feel-good hormone that elevates our ability to communicate, collaborate and trust others by activating networks in our prefrontal cortex. But oxytocin metabolizes more quickly than cortisol, so its effects are less dramatic and long-lasting.*
>
> *"This "chemistry of conversations" is why it's so critical for all of us –especially managers – to be more mindful about our interactions. Behaviors that increase cortisol levels reduce what I call "Conversational Intelligence" or "C-IQ," or a person's ability to connect and think innovatively, empathetically, creatively and strategically with others. Behaviors that spark oxytocin, by contrast, raise C-IQ."* [10]

THE LINK TO THE COACHING CYCLE

My suggested first step in the "coaching cycle" is to make positive assumptions about the individual whom you are coaching. Why? Because they feel your assumptions! Whatever comes out of your mouth is very likely to be colored, in words or tone, by the assumptions you make about

---

[10] Harvard Business Review Blog. *"The Neurochemistry of Positive Conversations"* Judith E. Glaser and Richard D. Glaser. JUNE 12, 2014

the other person. The act of making positive assumptions is almost like delivering one dose of an oxytocin pill (metaphorically speaking, of course!)

Modeling the desired behavior, practicing, and providing positive reinforcement in the form of verbal approval, provides a second dose of oxytocin. Each dose "opens" a person's ability to learn, or as Judith Glaser says, *"a person's ability to connect and think innovatively, empathetically, creatively."* This is at the heart of continuous improvement, isn't it?

This also sheds light on Dr. Deming's admonition to "drive out fear." Why? Because fear, caused by negative assumptions and negative interactions, produce higher levels of cortisol. It is interesting that cortisol acts as a "slow release tablet" with a longer lasting effect than that of oxytocin.[11]

From a hereditary, evolutionary psychology perspective this is likely because one mistake (I walked down that path and a tiger jumped out and almost ate me!) had far more lasting effects than positive outcomes (I walked down the path and saw a beautiful sunset.) Hence, it may be argued that we have a biological need for "Four-to-One" just to stay in balance in terms of our openness to learning and creativity.

What a coach does is not so much to provide direction, "right answers", but rather to open the person to thinking or meditating about their own behavior, and they thereby discover the lessons to be learned. Going back to the very beginning of lean/TPS development, this is what Toyota's Shigeo Shingo did with the stamping press team to reduce die change set up time. He didn't provide answers or solutions, he merely provided the data and asked questions.

It may be useful for managers to understand that their own behavior is having a bio-chemical effect on the brains of their subordinates. To put it bluntly, by creating fear they are likely making their subordinates behave in less intelligent ways - continuously improving stupidity! Creating stupidity

---

[11] *Oxytocin: Oxytocin is a powerful hormone. When we hug or kiss a loved one, oxytocin levels drive up. It also acts as a neurotransmitter in the brain. In fact, the hormone plays a huge role in pair bonding. Prairie voles, one of nature's most monogamous species, produce oxytocin in spades. This hormone is also greatly stimulated during sex, birth, breast feeding—the list goes on. (http://www.psychologytoday.com/basics/oxytocin).*

is the contrary model to that which we need to build lean organizations. We need more "conversational intelligence."

CHAPTER 9

MOTIVATION AND THE LEAN COACH

A coach will, at times, need to address the motivation of both individual leaders and teams. The simple act of asking questions, like those in the coaching maps (see Part Three), can serve to motivate individuals and teams to action. Encouragement or positive reinforcement serves to motivate. But the organization is a system and that system itself serves to motivate or demotivate individuals. The following is an effort to present the system of motivation at Toyota and other lean companies. It may be helpful as the coach analyzes his or her own organization's systems. [12]

**

One aspect of lean that has not been given enough attention, in my opinion, is how lean is an organization-wide system of motivation that creates a high performing culture. Too many lean implementations suffer from a focus on problem-solving skills, but a failure to attend to the system or culture of motivation. Too many rely on the *"they really oughtta wanna"* assumption which usually results in disappointment.

COMPETENCY X MOTIVATION = PERFORMANCE

Ultimately all organization's performance comes down to human behavior. There are always two aspects to achieving high performance: one is competence and the other is motivation. There must be competence in technical skills and there must be competence in social skills such as teamwork and problem-solving, for example. But, skills are useless unless individuals are motivated to use them. From my experience in high performing organizations, there is a high degree of motivation, for not only personal success, but the collective success of the group - the team and the

[12] This chapter was previously published in the Management Meditations blog.

company. Many of those implementing lean would do well to focus more on creating a systematic approach to motivating all members of the organization.

There are dozens of theories and hundreds of books on motivation. Without entering into a debate about different theories it is best to recognize that people are motivated by different things at different times, and in different circumstances. Some are motivated by a higher calling and some are motivated by money. In experimental psychology there is the idea of *multiple schedules of reinforcement*. This simply means that at the same time we may be motivated by long-term career goals, a desire to serve our family, money, and social recognition by team members. Multiple things are reinforcing (or punishing) our behavior at the same time, and our behavior is a result of the net effects of these different stimuli. Focusing on only one source motivation (or schedule of reinforcement) is a mistake. It is better to optimize all of the forms of motivation and thereby impact the most number of people who each have their own personal desires.

The job of management is to optimize all of the available sources of motivation to increase those behaviors that contribute to the success of the organization.

It is useful to think of three types or sources of motivation: 1) purpose or meaning; 2) social relationships, and 3) situational rewards and punishment. You can think of these as a hierarchy from the spiritual to the

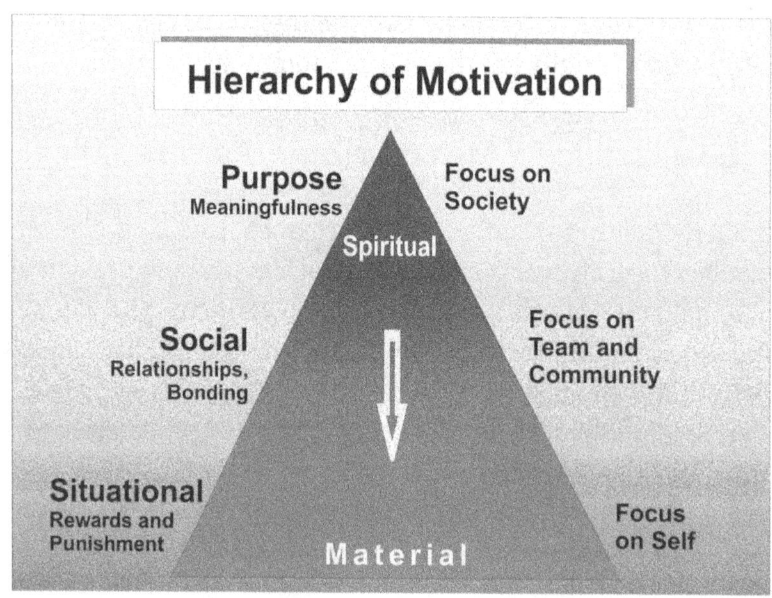

material. I suggest not judging that one is better than another. If you are starving, getting a meal is very important. At different times in our life each form of motivation may be more or less important. However, I would make the value judgement that being focused only on the material or the self is a weakness. There is a great deal of research that demonstrates that we are happier human beings when we are focused on serving others, working in groups, and when we feel that our lives are achieving an ennobling purpose.

Let's look at each of these and see how they may be optimized in your organization.

THE PURPOSE PRINCIPLE

Every human being searches for life's meaning - a spiritual attraction to a higher purpose, something beyond the self or immediate gratification. Your religious faith, your family, and your country may all be sources of motivation at this spiritual level. Motives at this level are almost always focused on the very long-term. You will sacrifice for achieving a goal in the afterlife. You will sacrifice much of your own pleasure for the well-being of your family. And many have willingly sacrificed their own lives for their country and their faith. When someone sacrifices for that which they believe to be noble we consider them more noble. Think of the last time you sacrificed your time, your energy or your money toward that which you believed to be noble. How did you feel? More noble. This is the inherent mystery of sacrifice and every great leader knows to call upon this human attraction to a higher purpose.

There was a period of few years back when there was a lot of focus on company mission, vision and values. It even became a source of jokes or references to "that vision thing." Of course lofty statements that are not supported by action, and by aligning processes and systems will soon become meaningless. But these statements can and should be a reference point for everything we do in the organization, just as the "right to freedom of speech, press and religion" can be a long-term and sustaining value for a country.

In healthcare and other organizations that provide direct human services, it is relatively easy to understand a "higher purpose" to your work. When manufacturing products it is a bit more difficult, but the world's best manufacturers are still able to create this sense of mission or purpose.

Both Toyota and Honda have given a great deal of thought to their mission, vision and values and they sincerely strive to put these into practice. In each case they do provide their associates with a sense of making a contribution, doing something worthy, beyond the pursuit of personal rewards.

TOYOTA'S GLOBAL VISION

"Toyota will lead the way to the future of mobility, enriching lives around the world with the safest and most responsible ways of moving people. Through our commitment to quality, constant innovation and respect for the planet, we aim to exceed expectations and be rewarded with a smile. We will meet our challenging goals by engaging the talent and passion of people, who believe there is always a better way."

HONDA'S GLOBAL VISION

Honda's "Fundamental Beliefs" are divided into "Respect for the Individual" and include Equality, Initiative and Trust. And, their "Three Joys" which are all based on how different stakeholders are made to feel by the actions and products of the corporation. I think it is easy for any employee to visualize each of these joys and answer the question "why are we doing this anyway?"

HONDA'S THREE JOYS

- ***The Joy of Buying***
  The joy of buying is achieved through providing products and services that exceed the needs and expectations of each customer.

- ***The Joy of Selling***
  The joy of selling occurs when those who are engaged in selling and servicing Honda products develop relationships with a customer based on mutual trust. Through this relationship, Honda associates, dealers and distributors experience pride

and joy in satisfying the customer and in representing Honda to the customer.

- ***The Joy of Creating***
  The joy of creating occurs when Honda associates and suppliers involved in the design, development, engineering and manufacturing of Honda products recognize a sense of joy in our customers and dealers. The joy of creating occurs when quality products exceed expectations and we experience pride in a job well done.

How Do You Make Use of Your Purpose?

If these statements are developed and stuck on the wall they will soon have little meaning. Here are some ways you can employ your purpose to achieve greater motivation:

- Every communication regarding strategies and objectives should make reference to how those strategies and objectives serve to achieve the company's purpose.
- When developing strategy and objectives your purpose should serve as a required point of reference.
- Each time executives give talks or presentations to employees they should frame the presentation in terms of the company purpose.
- When discussing quality problems, you can refer to the purpose. For example, "how do you think this will impact the joy of selling or buying our car?"

The Motivation of Social Bonds

The United States has long been torn between the appeal of rugged individualism and the desire for community. Much of our mythology is built around the idea of the Lone Ranger, the lone entrepreneur, or the individual (Horatio Alger) who achieves great wealth fighting against great odds. The reality of our entrepreneurial culture is that it is built on both. The New World was settled by small Pilgrim groups who came and settled in what were essentially communes. We moved West in wagon trains, not single wagons, and those wagon trains formed large circles at night to provide the protection of the group. And, our early history was one of farming communities who worked as a group to build barns and formed farm collectives to purchase supplies and market their products. And, our industry also started in small craft shops that were essentially family units. One can make a good argument that we have a genetic predisposition to work in small groups. Our genetic ancestors hunting antelope on the Serengeti Plains of Africa hunted in family groups, teams and they would have starved hunting alone.

Research has demonstrated that those who have close social bonds - family, community or church - are likely to be happier, have fewer incidents of depression and live longer. Those who live in isolation suffer the reverse. It is not surprising that when Henry Ford's factory broke the work down into highly specialized, individualized and isolated tasks, workers suffered depression and ultimately rebelled by self-organizing into groups in which they called each other brothers. The cause of unionization was not just money. It was the psychological need for human bonding, a team, a union, or a gang in the inner city, all serve to create a family-like unit that provides psychological safety.

The importance of the team process in the Toyota Production System has been undervalued. The work team at Toyota and Honda are equivalent

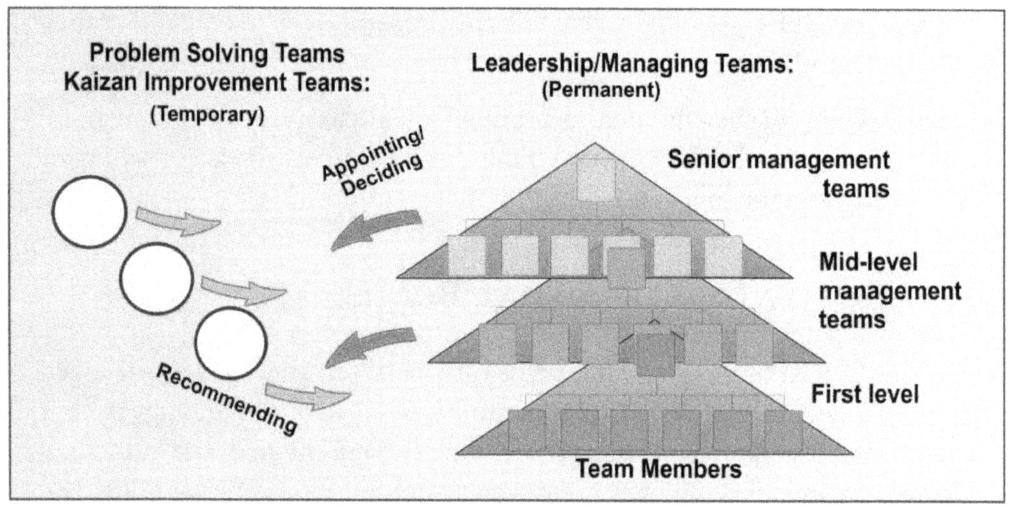

to the family unit in society. It is the primary learning organization, the primary source of bonding with a group, and the primary way employees contribute to the company's mission. The work team is at the Gemba! But many companies make the mistake of assuming that the formation of work teams is the sole solution to creating a team culture. After more than thirty years of implementing self-directed work teams I can promise that if managers are not formed into teams, trained in the exact same team skills and processes, the team culture will not take hold. Teams must be effective at every level.

Problem-solving teams have often been assumed to be the essential types of teams associated with lean management. This is an error! Problem-solving teams are formed to address problems that cut across teams or functions and which cannot be solved within a work team. The natural work team is where employees are empowered to think and solve problems on a daily basis. It is in the daily huddle where a ten minute PDCA cycle can solve problems quickly by those who are most expert in their work.

Jeff Liker and Michael Hoseus in their book *Toyota Culture* well describe the importance of the work team and the team leader:

> *"At Toyota there are small rewards at the team level and the potential of more significant bonuses shared by everyone if the plant and company perform well. Delving deeper into the values and assumptions of the Toyota culture, we can see this approach reflects the value placed on teamwork. More broadly, Toyota wants its team members to develop the highest level of accountability and ownership and as such to understand that their fate is tied to the company." (p. 8-9)*
>
> *"It is interesting that the team leader within Toyota is considered the lynch pin of TPS and few companies 'going lean' have this role... It is safe to say that the Toyota Production System would not function without high performance teams on the shop floor." (p. 228)*

What defines a group of people as a high performance team? If I were to walk through your facility, I would randomly speak to employees and ask them the following questions which define a high performing team:

- Do you have on-going responsibility for a work process that results in business revenue, operating costs or meets customer and client satisfaction requirements. What is that process?
- Do you know your customers who value your work and do you communicate with them concerning their requirements and satisfaction?

- Do you have a balanced scorecard that includes process, finance, customer satisfaction and learning or development measures?
- Do you have daily or weekly meetings in which you review your performance and solve problems?
- Do you have the responsibility to evaluate your performance, solve problems and make decisions to continuously improve your operations?
- Do you have a visual display of your team's performance?
- Has your team been coached in team skills, and have they demonstrated competence in each of the above tasks?

Situational Motivation

Situational motivation is the result of the reinforcement or punishment of behavior. Acknowledging that many of us are motivated on a personal level by various forms of recognition for our own behavior should in no way negate the importance of the previous two forms of motivation. Motivation is not a zero sum game, it is additive.

It is important to recognize that when both Honda and Toyota built plants in the United States they both changed their systems of motivation. They both adopted the "American way" of individual initiative and the individual desire for recognition. Neither of them said "The Japanese way is best and you Americans must adopt it." On the contrary, they redesigned their systems to adapt to the American culture. This is an important lesson.

"Toyota has a strong philosophy of teamwork, sharing rewards and expecting people to do their best for the company. They did not want to compromise these principles when they expanded to North America. At the same time, they had to understand and respect the realities of Western culture." (p. 400) Toyota Culture.

To adapt to this culture Toyota developed a different compensation system. *"The philosophy and much of the practice of compensating salaried members is the same as for hourly employees. The base salary is approximately 75% of the total with the other 25% variable pay in the form of bonuses." (Ibid., p 407)*

At Honda America Manufacturing they developed a point system, much like one I implemented in a North Carolina prison setting many years before (see the Case Study later in this book).

One day some years back I was visiting the Honda Marysville plant and I observed an award ceremony in which an individual employee was being awarded a Honda Civic, which he earned by accumulating individual points. The Quality Circle program, suggestion system, quality awards, and safety awards are all tied together with a point system that is awarded individually. Every associate earns points by participating in any of these improvement processes. Awards include award certificates, gift certificates, Department Manager's Award, Plant Manager's Award, and President's Award. These also result in points accumulating over your career, and can earn a Honda Civic (that was for 2,500 points, at the time of my visit) and an Accord (5,000 points), plus two weeks off with pay and airplane tickets to anywhere in the world with spending money. Good attendance results in another bonus.

In addition to hourly or salaried compensation, all associates participate in profit sharing. This profit sharing is an innovation of Honda of America and is not part of the system in Japan. Ten percent of the gross profit generated by Honda Motor Company is shared with associates based on their relative compensation.

In your organization, are there multiple ways, as at Honda, for individuals to earn both tangible and social recognition for individual efforts that contribute to the success of the company? Ask yourself the following question about the consequence for good performance in your organization:

- *If an individual or a team set a new record for productivity, what happens? How is this behavior reinforced?*
- *Have managers, particularly team leaders, been trained in the skill of providing feedback?*
- *Does your organization practice "four-to-one", four positive consequences or comments by managers to each one negative?*
- *How are creative suggestions that result in savings or improved performance positively reinforced?*

- *Are employees more motivated by opportunities to "win" (best attendance, most suggestions, best team of the month, etc.) or by the fear of negative consequences for failure?*

It Is A System - Not An Event or Accident!

A highly motivated work force is not an accident. It is not the result of being in one part of the country or another, having a union or not having a union. It is the result of systematic efforts on the part of management to design and improve a system of motivation. The most effective systems optimize both an ennobling purpose, the social bonds of strong teamwork, and the availability of individual incentives. They all contribute unique elements to a holistic system of motivation.

Chapter 10

Coaching to Optimize Team Self-Control

Many organizations are not gaining the potential benefits of teams in the workplace due to the failure to optimize team autonomy and self-control. This is a critical issue in organization design and leadership today, particular in non-manufacturing organizations such as healthcare or information technology. When teams gain self-control they require less management, are more motivated and will be more creative in their improvement efforts.

Do Autonomous or Self-Managed Teams Exist?

Many labels have been used to describe teams in the work place: high performing teams, self-directed, self-managing, autonomous or semi-autonomous, or self-sustaining teams. More simply... just work teams, work cells, work groups or management teams.

My associates and I have trained many thousands of teams and team leaders in about one hundred companies. I can honestly say that in all that time I have never seen an absolutely self-managed team (or self-directed or autonomous). So long as there is a Board of Directors, the senior management team is not self-managed. As long as there is a plant manager, hospital administrator, or any other manager, front line teams are not self-managed. As long as there is a spouse... you're not either! Terms such as *self-managed* are absolute, and absolutes are never absolutely true. This term can lead to unfortunate confusion among team members. There are, however, degrees of autonomy or self-direction.

Motivation and Team Autonomy

Why does team autonomy matter? It matters for several reasons, and each of these reasons are tied to achieving a high performing organization.

- First, it is in our nature to move from the dependent relationships of childhood to the increasingly independent relationships of adolescence. And then, to the interdependent relationships of marriage and maturity. It is demotivating, whether at work or in the family, to be restricted to a dependent condition. Dependence leads to helplessness, which leads to depression, which equals a lack of motivation. The infant is naturally motivated to crawl, to explore, and expand their circle of control. Authoritarian organizations assume the dependence of the level below, rather than encouraging greater autonomy. By unnecessarily restricting autonomy they destroy the natural forces of motivation.
- Creativity, entrepreneurship and continuous improvement are all connected to degrees of autonomy and the acceptance of responsibility. If you feel dependent on the decisions of others, you are less likely to think about ways to improve. If you believe in your own empowerment, or the self-control of your team, you are more likely to engage in the mental activity of thinking about ways to improve.
- Mastery and self-learning are linked to autonomy. If your job is to simply do what you are told, there is little incentive to either be creative, or to seek mastery of current or new skills. A belief in your self-determination will increase your desire to seek self-mastery of those skills that will lead to your success.

The Autonomy Matrix

The following matrix may be helpful in explaining the progress toward both autonomy and high performance. The vertical axis describes the degree of team maturity and skill. The greater the maturity and skill, the greater the justification for autonomy. The horizontal axis describes who decides and who solves problems. To the left, the manager decides and controls, to the right the team decides and controls.

1A: In quadrant 1A the manager recognizes that the team is not yet mature or lacks skills; she is directive and makes most decisions. If you leave the team in this quadrant they will lose motivation. This should be viewed as only an early stage of development for a team.

1B: In this quadrant the leader has turned over control to the team, but the team has not sufficiently matured to accept this responsibility. This is somewhat like the permissive parent who gives control to his teenage son who is not ready to accept responsibility. Poor performance is likely to result. Hold on to the car keys!

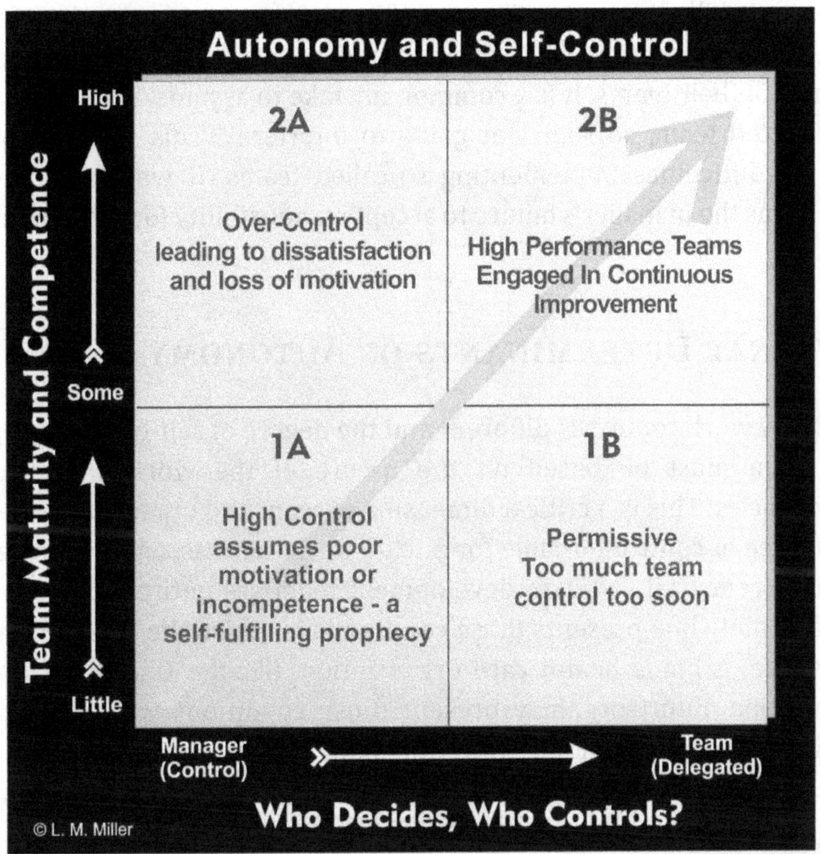

2A: In this quadrant the team has developed the skills and maturity but the manager won't let go. This over-control hinders the development of the team and may result in the "rebellious teenager." Teams may rebel against over control, but the team members will soon lose motivation.

2B: In the Northeast quadrant the team is skilled and mature and the manager has delegated decision-making and a high degree of control to the team. Achieving this state of maturity results in a highly motivated team, rapid improvement cycles, and a reduced need (cost) for management doing non-value-adding work.

The goal of development is to move smoothly from 1A to 2B. However, as every parent knows, developing a team to maturity, just like developing a child to adulthood, is rarely a straight line. There is always testing of control limits and failures to behave maturely. Rather than halt progress, these deviations should be viewed as inevitable experimentation on the way to maturity.

As the skilled parent is "sensitive" to the degree of maturity of their child, the manager must be sensitive and respond appropriately to the maturity of their teams. It is a common mistake to assume "Well, they are a self-directed team, so I am not going to interfere!" This was one of the common difficulties implementing so-called teams. It wasn't the team's fault. It was the manager's failure to accept responsibility for developing the team.

External Determinants of Autonomy

Every work context is different and the degree of self-control assigned to a team must be based on the nature of the work and external dependencies. This is a critical dimension of team and organization design. The degree of control possible for a team on an auto assembly line versus an entrepreneurial software development team are entirely different. An auto assembly line presents those conditions in which the least autonomy is possible. A home health care organization, like the Danish healthcare organization Buurtzorg, may present those conditions with the highest possible degree of autonomy while still being part of a larger organization.

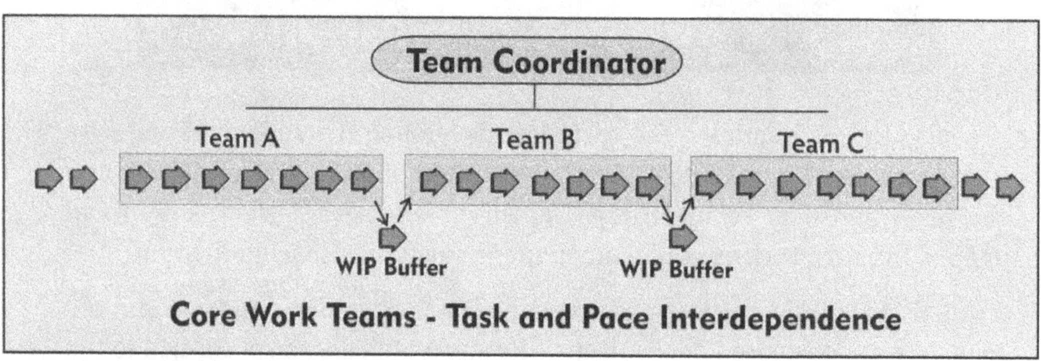

Core Work Teams - Task and Pace Interdependence

Here are some of the determinants of autonomy:

1. The pace and content of work may be determined by prior and subsequent teams. On an auto assembly line, from which a great deal of lean thinking has derived, there is a very high level of interdependence, both in pace and content of work between each team. Team "B" in the above illustration, cannot make a decision to increase their pace of work if the prior and subsequent teams do not also increase their pace. The work-in-process (WIP) buffer is minimized in lean manufacturing to reduce waste. The less buffer, the greater the need for a pace of work identical to the previous and subsequent teams. They cannot simply decide to add or remove tasks or parts without that decision impacting other teams. They are going to have a low degree of autonomy dictated by this external dependency.
2. A contrary example is a software development team, or a group of software development teams, that may have some degree of interdependence. A group of high school friends who get together to develop an IOS app on the weekends can be very independent

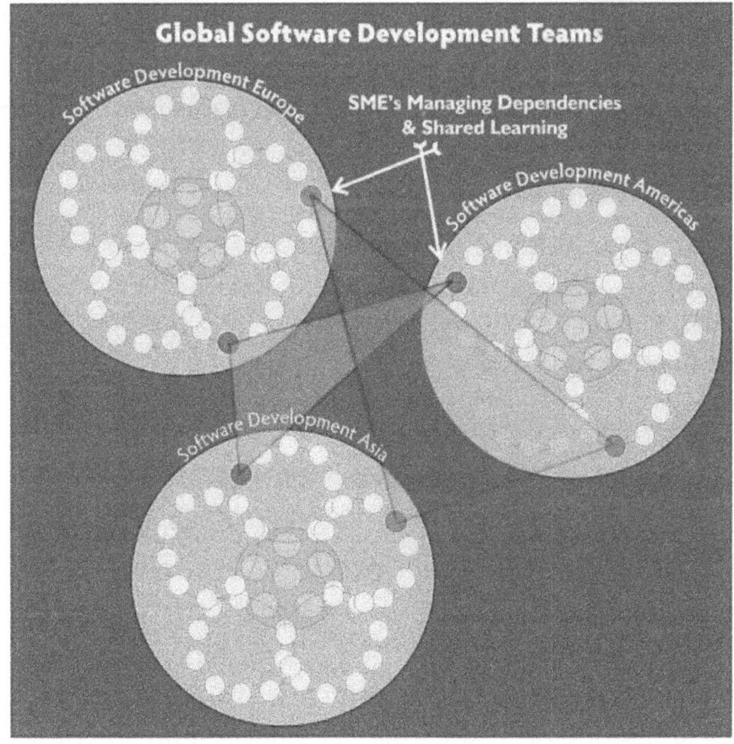

and self-directed. On the other hand, a global accounting firm developing software for their global accounting clients may have teams working in different parts of the world. These teams may be much more self-directed than the auto assembly line, but they share dependencies, such as common software language, common clients, common accounting language and algorithms. These teams may have subject matter experts to manage specific dependencies across teams.

Internal Determinants of Autonomy

Many of the determinants of the ability of a team to function successfully with a high degree of autonomy are internal to the team – both in its design and its development. Here are a few of those factors:

- Development of decision-making and problem-solving skills: Too often teams are not provided with the training to enable them to solve problems well. This may then cause managers to feel that the team is not willing to assume responsibility. The manager must distinguish between "can't do" versus "won't do" limitations.
- Selection of team members: Personalities can play a role in the success of any team at any level. This is one reason for engaging the team in self-selection of team members. This can enhance their acceptance of responsibility for each other's success.
- Data presentation: Like athletic teams, all teams need data and the system must provide that data. Is data provided to the team in a visual manner, at a high frequency (hourly or daily?) requiring little administrative time?
- Tools: Are all the necessary tools available in the team's work area?
- Complete skill sets to match the work: if you are designing a baseball team you know that the skills of pitching, playing shortstop, and other positions are necessary for the team to be successful. The same is true on any work team. Are these defined in the design?
- Decision Authority: What decision authority has been designed into the team process? Consider the responsibility of Toyota workers to pull the Andon cord that stops the assembly line. This is decision

authority assigned to individual workers. It has a huge impact on how they think and feel about their work.

- Motivation Systems: What rewards and recognition are available to reinforce a team successfully achieving goals?
- Knowledge Access: What knowledge do they have access to that will enhance their work and decision-making? Imagine the effect of Google search on almost every job. We can eliminate waste and reduce the need for reaching out or up, if we have access to required information. Optimize this access!

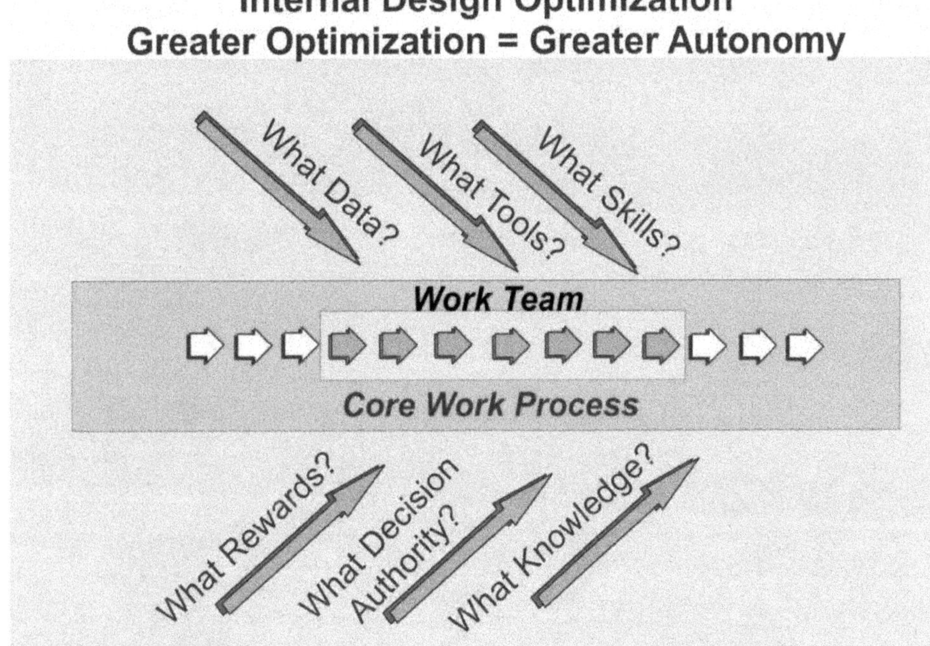

You can probably think of other internal and external determinants of autonomy. As a coach you should consider the design of the system of organization and the work process. These often limit autonomy and motivation. The degree of team autonomy and self-direction, while never complete, will be a major factor in the success of your organization.

Chapter 11

How to Build a Lean System of Organizational Learning

The world of corporate training and development has yet to fully embrace the new reality of technology, online resources, and the need to integrate learning into the daily habits of all managers and team members.

Just as colleges and universities are struggling to confront out-of-control costs and the integration of new technology, corporate training and development must also adopt a new paradigm to deliver competence and capabilities to their customers.

Lean Systems of Corporate Training

In 2015 Forbes Magazine published their annual research on corporate training. In 2014 spending increased 15% to $70 billion in the US and $130 billion worldwide. The number one area of spending is on management and leadership development, at 35%. That equals $24.5 Billion in the U.S. and $45.5 Billion worldwide for management and leadership development training.

Why? Forbes stated:

> *"All our research on corporate talent shows that global leadership gaps continue to be the most pressing issues on the minds of business and HR leaders. As Millennials take on more responsibility, companies need to build leadership skills at all levels and in all geographies around the world."*

Two other significant findings by Forbes: High performing companies spend more on training and technology is revolutionizing this market.

> *"The research shows an explosive growth in technology tools to train people today. Self-authored video, online communication channels,*

virtual learning, (Coursera, Udacity, Udemy, edX, ...) are all growing rapidly as training tools. People still need formal classroom education, but this is now less than half the total "hours" people consume in training around the world. And among the highly advanced companies, as much as 18% of all training is now delivered through mobile devices."

The New World of Training and Development

So, what is the problem? The problem is that much of these expenditures are anything but "lean." Specifically:

- Many corporate trainers, internal and external, are wedded to the old model - "Send them to me and I will talk and they will do exercises, we'll have great coffee breaks, go home, and it is their problem what happens after that. I've done my job!" In other words, it is "silo-ed" and lacking a continuous process flow that begins with a defined need and ends in proof of performance.
- Leaders send subordinates to training and expect them to be "fixed," with little acceptance of responsibility for coaching and observing demonstrated competence in a defined skill.
- Learners go to training or watch online courses with little understanding that they are responsible for performing, demonstrating competence, and adding value. This is not their fault. It is the fault of the system - the absence of accountability and consequences.
- The solution is a system that creates value and returns the investment, which must include the following elements: Line managers must define, with the help of training professionals, competency-based training that builds specific skills that will then be used and coached on the job.
- Participation in online learning, whether through internal learning management systems or services like Udemy, should not simply be a do-it-yourself "go watch this and learn something" model. On the contrary, courses should be watched on the individual's time, but an entire team of managers should participate together, with an internal coach facilitating the application of learning in the real world environment. Learning comes from doing, not watching!!

- It is a new, but old, paradigm. Learning must be managed and not left to chance. Each manager must be responsible (that means held accountable) for the development of her people. They must be given a system of learning for which they can be responsible.

A System of Organizational Learning

Let me suggest how a "lean" learning system might work. The purpose of this model is to both incorporate the efficiency of online learning technology, while at the same time understanding that learning occurs through applied action, iterative experimentation, coaching (feedback) and consequences to behavior.

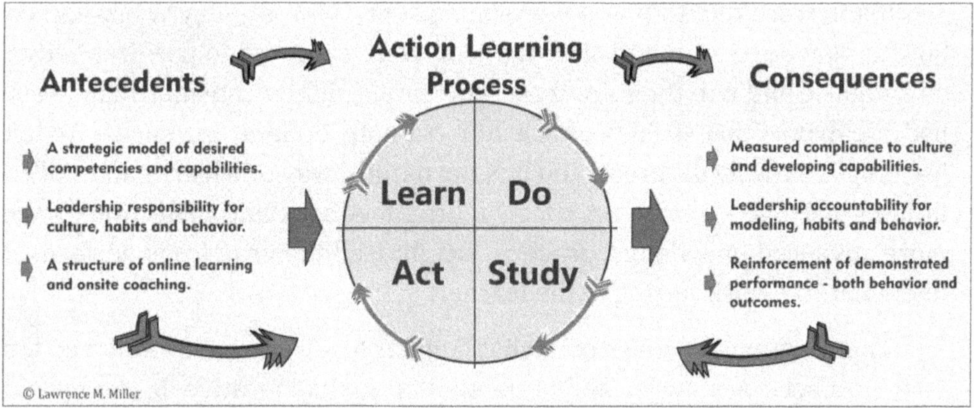
Antecedents
A strategic model of desired competencies and capabilities.
Leadership responsibility for culture, habits and behavior.
A structure of online learning and onsite coaching.
Action Learning Process
Learn
Do
Act
Study
Consequences
Measured compliance to culture and developing capabilities.
Leadership accountability for modeling, habits and behavior.
Reinforcement of demonstrated performance - both behavior and outcomes.
© Lawrence M. Miller

Antecedents

Organization leadership has the responsibility to establish the conditions for purposeful learning. These include the following:

- *A Strategic Capability Model that Defines Cultural Competencies:* Where are we going, why, and what capabilities do we need to get there? Organizational learning is not an act of personal fulfillment. It must be made purposeful by a strategic model that defines the capabilities, technical and social, that the organization must possess to succeed in the future.
- *Leadership Responsibility:* Just as each unit of the business is held accountable for budget items, achieving targets of productivity or

sales, the same business unit leaders must be equally responsible for building the human capabilities that will lead to the fulfillment of strategy.

- *Structure and Systems*: To establish a system of learning, the structure, systems and tools must be put in place by leadership. The online learning system needs to be established or purchased. The structure of internal coaches who will follow up and counsel managers on their application of lessons learned in online programs is essential to the process.

The Action-Learning Process

If you were told that you were being sent to a three-day workshop on how to play the guitar, and after that you were expected to perform before an audience and win their applause, you would rightly consider that a very bad idea! But, that is how much our training dollars are spent. Action learning is entirely different, and it is the natural way one learns any skill: a little knowledge - a little practice - a little feedback and reflection - then more advanced knowledge, practice, etc. And, all the practice is performed in the natural work setting of the learner.

This diagram will look somewhat familiar to all who have employed the Plan-Do-Check-Act cycle, and it is similar in its iterative learning and experimentation process. However, it is adapted specifically to management and leadership development.

1. Learn: Acquire Knowledge

In traditional learning models this is where most of the time, attention and costs went. No longer. This is the easy part. This is where online learning changes everything. To use my own course as an example, the individual can learn the problem-solving models, process management, the skill of developing scoreboards, solving human performance problems, and facilitation skills while sitting at home in the evening or at Starbucks on

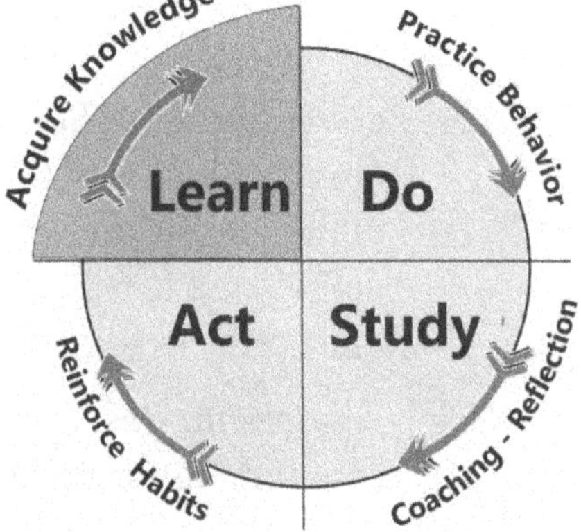

their tablet. The knowledge is all there. In the case of my team leadership course, there are 17 hours of lectures broken into 74 separate lectures. It is enough for one full year of management development when combined with the other three elements.

2. Do: Practice the Behavior

To take the example of learning a language or musical instrument, as anyone who has tried knows, the essential step in real learning is building the habits through practice. Learning management and leadership skills are no different. Effective communication and facilitation, for example, is a skill comprised of a set of habits. We know what those habits are. The knowledge is relatively simple. But, developing the habitual behavior of listening well, inquiring sincerely before judging, or acknowledging the contribution of others, is less about knowledge than habit.

Where does the manager practice these skills? The best place is right where he or she works - in their own work or management team. One might expect this to be uncomfortable. However, if the team is learning together, all trying out new behavior, the performance anxiety is minimized.

3. Study: Coaching & Reflection

Leadership skills are developed, through a period of years, by acquiring knowledge, doing and coaching. However, while almost every company is striving to adopt lean manufacturing or culture, few are taking coaching seriously. There is something in our culture that causes us to say "I'm OK, I can do it myself, I don't need a coach!" Tom Brady has a coach. Peyton Manning has a coach. But our managers too often think they don't need one!

Coaching is giving feedback on the performance of a specific skill. It is not asking the same questions repeatedly. It is asking questions about the application of the specific skill the learner is practicing at that time. A skilled coach follows a learning path in support of the acquisition of knowledge, and the sequence of practice. As an example, I have defined a sequence of activities and related coaching questions that follow my *Team Leadership* course. (See the Coaching Maps in Part Three of this book.)

4. Act: To Reinforce Habits

It is the responsibility of leaders to reinforce habits that comprise the capabilities that will lead to strategic success. Ultimately, you get what you reward!

It is unfortunate that many leaders do not see the connection between reinforcing those skills for which the organization is providing training, and achieving a return on those training dollars. I can't tell you how many times I have seen a huge investment in culture change efforts, only to see the promotion of someone who everyone knew had displayed behavior contrary to that which the leaders professed to support. Nothing is more discouraging.

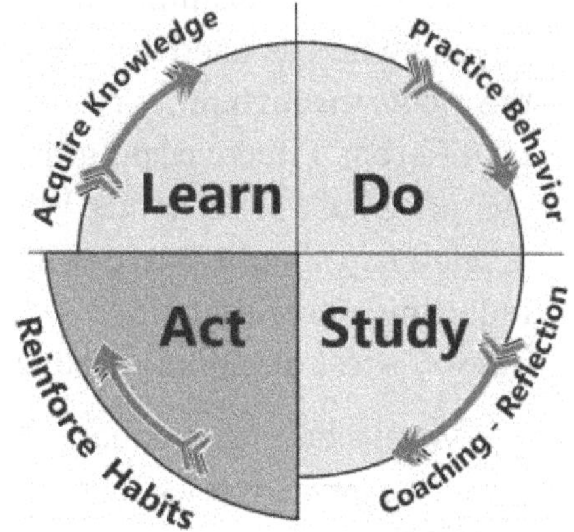

When a critical mass of the organization's members have learned new management skills, those management practices become standard work. They should be identified as a component of a competency model for that job. Then they become part of the culture.

Consequences

Ever since my early days setting up a free economy behind prison walls, I have been a great believer in the power of consequences to influence behavior. The culture of training and development was, for too long, one in which measurement of outcomes, changes in behavior and performance, were not viewed as part of the trainer's job. Trainers were comfortable in the silo of training departments, were content to hand-off a trained individual to line management, and considered their job complete. This separation of training and performance creates waste! This silo must be broken.

- *Measure Cultural Competence:* Leadership and management training can demonstrate changes in behavior on the job. I have long had assessments and accountability measures for training in team leadership and lean leadership skills. Those measures include the direct application of the skills to improve operating performance.

- *Leadership Accountability for Modeling Behavior*: If you want your managers to practice good process management or problem-solving skills, the leaders must model that behavior. Only that modeling will demonstrate its importance and instill the belief that those skills pay off.
- *Reinforce Demonstrated Performance:* Those implementing lean management have largely ducked the issue of reward systems. Why? Rewarding desired behavior gets you more desired behavior. Yes, it can sometimes be complicated or not perfectly fair. No reward system is. But, in one Merck plant, for example, as they went through the team leadership training, a set of deliverables were identified, and the annual plant bonus, for both salaried and hourly employees, was tied to the completion of those deliverables. It was a strong motivator!

Whether you agree with all of the elements of the system proposed above is not critical. What is critical is that we rethink the system of learning in our organizations to eliminate waste and gain maximum benefit. I believe the above elements will move most organizations in that direction.

Chapter 12

Dr. Deming's Joy, Happiness & the Lean Organization

The lean coach may become extremely focused on quality and productivity data, cycle times and other key performance indicators. However, there is a soft side that is also worthy of attention.

> *"Management's overall aim should be to create a system in which everybody may take joy in his work."* Dr. W. Edwards Deming

The cynic may picture workers sitting around with a drink in hand, party hats, and dancing around the workplace in a silly display of "joy." But, obviously that is not what Deming was promoting. He was promoting the need and possibility of intrinsic reinforcement, joy from the job itself, the achievement, the self-satisfaction derived from the ability to improve and control one's own work.

At some time, you have most likely experienced joy in your work. Whenever I have asked clients to identify the time they felt most joy in their work, they are likely to describe a time when they were engaged in meeting a challenge and succeeding. That challenge might be learning a new job or developing and implementing a new process or product. Alternatively, they may point to a time when they were working with a great team of colleagues who shared the same goal and determination. In other words, they were not partying, they were performing. Great parties are quickly forgotten; great performance is long remembered.

Dr. Deming's instruction was based more on his own excellent intuition than on any research. However, in the past twenty years, the most popular area of psychological research has been *positive psychology,* which is simply the study of psychological wellness, rather than illness. The first book I read on this subject was *Authentic Happiness* by Martin Seligman and I highly recommend it. Since its publication, there has been a flood of happiness books. I would encourage you to explore Dr. Seligman's Authentic Happiness website, where you can take a survey to find out how happy you are while at the same time contributing to his research database.

So, what is the big finding of positive psychology?

"The belief that we can rely on shortcuts to happiness, joy, rapture, comfort, and ecstasy, rather than be entitled to these feelings by the exercise of personal strengths and virtues, leads to legions of people who in the middle of great wealth are starving spiritually. Positive emotions alienated from the exercise of character leads to emptiness, to in-authenticity, to depression, and, as we age, to the gnawing realization that we are fidgeting until we die."[13]

In other words, if eating chocolate sundaes, sex and money resulted in authentic happiness you would find the happiest people to be those who have the most money, sex and ice cream. However, that simply is not so. They are more likely to be the most depressed and anxious. What does lead to happiness is knowledge of your strengths, developing and exercising those strengths; and exercising the virtues of character and strong social relationships. People who have a strong community of relatives and friends are happier than those who have few friends and only distant relatives. Those who are optimistic and have hope in achieving a positive goal are happier than those who are pessimistic or feeling helpless.

Coaching Toward Happiness

If you read many of the books about happiness that are based on research, you will find that there is a consensus view regarding the key factors that lead to a happy life, and each of them has direct implications for creating a happy and productive relationships at work. Here they are:

1. Strong Social Relationships Lead to Joy

Forty percent of those who are married say they are "very happy", while only 24 percent of those who are not married report being very happy. That advantage holds for men and women, young and old. Very happy people spend the most time in socializing, and the least time alone. People who are very sociable, good conversationalists, good listeners, tend

---

[13] Seligman, Martin E.P. Authentic Happiness. Free Press, New York, 2002. P.8.

to be happier and more likely to be married. It is hard to separate cause from effect because each of these factors reinforces the others. In other words, if you are more sociable you are more likely to be married, and the reverse is true.

Religious belief and participation in a religious community strongly correlates with happiness. Religious Americans are less likely to abuse drugs, get divorced, commit crimes, or kill themselves. They are also physically healthier and live longer. There are several possible causes. One is simply that a strong moral code or value system provides guidance that directs one to behavior that is more satisfying and less the cause of unhappiness. Another possible explanation is that religion is often the basis of community life and a strong social network.

What does this tell us about creating "joy at work?" It is most likely to come from a strong social network, teams and teamwork in the workplace. The family farm and early craft shops were organized on strong social relationship and provided security and happiness. The factories of mass production in which each worker was told to "do your own work", led to isolation and alienation. The formation of unions, in which they called each other "brothers", was a natural act of psychological survival. Now we know that creating natural brotherhoods and sisterhoods, social bonds in the workplace lead to both happiness and behavior that is more productive. Almost all innovation is the result of trusting relationships and teamwork.

It is the duty of the manager to assure that no one is alone in his or her work, and that everyone is a member of a supportive group, a social network or a team.

2. We Derive Joy from our Strengths

Playing tennis does not make me happy. Dancing does not make me happy. Why? Because I stink at those things. Playing the guitar, and more particularly, learning a new tune on the guitar, makes me very happy. As you might guess, I am a decent guitar player (at least in my own mind and I ask you not to interrupt that thought) and a student of folk blues guitar. We all have strengths, and a healthy workplace is composed of people with diverse strengths. Recognizing the value of that diversity, the contribution of each strength, provides an opportunity for joy. A great workplace is an orchestra comprised of individual competencies playing in harmony.

There is a close relationship between Toyota's principle of "respect for people" and Honda's principle that "the world's greatest experts are on-the-spot" and the joy that comes from building and using your strengths. In every workplace, every member of the organization deserves respect for his or her expertise. They should know that they are expert and have the dignity and the joy that comes from that self-awareness and from building that strength. On the other hand, in my guitar example, from learning a new tune. Learning, building on strengths, brings joy.

Does this mean that we should ignore weaknesses? No. If an employee is weak at showing up on time or at completing assigned work, those weaknesses need to be addressed. Weaknesses should not be our sole focus. Focusing only on solving problems can lead to an excessive focus on weakness and not on strengths. This is what makes for a joyful workplace.

Recently I was in a manufacturing plant in which many line production workers were trained to do only one repetitive job, and had been at it for many years. What do you think happens to the mind when someone does only one job and does it day after day, year after year? It is deadly. These same workers can be trained to do every job on the line. This increases the flexibility of the manufacturing process and increases every worker's ability to solve problems and improve the process. Multi-skilled workers are more valuable than single-skilled workers are. In addition, where does the joy come from? It comes to employees from being on an effective team and having developed multiple skills that allow him to help others in their work. The greater the ability to contribute to the team, the greater the self-worth of the individual.

3. Money Does Make You Happy… To A Point

One of the great myths of motivation is that money doesn't motivate. For some reason I always hear this from the person in the organization who makes the most money. It's rubbish! It is fair to assume that everyone is motivated to be happy. The question then is, "Does money make you happy?" Let me quote from Christopher Peterson's excellent book *Pursuing the Good Life:*

> *"Research shows that income has a positive relationship with happiness (life satisfaction), although it is not a straight line. As income increases, its added contribution to life satisfaction becomes smaller. The*

impact of additional income is greatest among those who have little money, but it does not stop mattering, even after someone is able to meet basic needs."

When the life satisfaction of people who live in poor countries is compared to those who live in wealthier nations there is a strong correlation of wealth to happiness. The least happy nations are the poorest. However, once a certain level of wealth is achieved, it matters little. As Seligman writes, "So, the Swiss are happier than the Bulgarians, but it hardly matters if one is Irish, Italian or American." Once a basic level of wealth is achieved, there is little gain in happiness above that.

In other words, if a manufacturing level employee can raise his or her income enough to be able to save for retirement and for a child's education, that increase does bring greater joy. The additional money has real utility. If the CEO of the company gets a raise from ten million dollars a year to eleven million dollars a year, after a day or two of self-congratulations, he will experience no greater happiness. In other words, corporate investment in high executive compensation is most often a lousy one in terms of happiness gained.

We also know that money, or any reward, affects behavior when there is a contingency, an if-then relationship between performance and money. You all have used "if you eat your vegetables, then you can have dessert." Similarly, if you study hard, you will get a good grade. Those are contingent relationships. Therefore, "f you learn these additional skills and can perform these additional job functions, you will earn X more per hour in compensation", does in fact motivate performance.

4. Altruism, Performing Work in the Spirit of Service, Makes You Happy

Ayn Rand (*Atlas Shrugged, The Fountainhead*) was wrong! In her promotion of the pseudo religion of *objectivism* she decried altruism and promoted self-interest as the highest ethic. She completely misunderstood altruism.

"What is the moral code of altruism? The basic principle of altruism is that man has no right to exist for his own sake, that service to others is the only justification of his existence, and that self-sacrifice is his highest moral duty, virtue and value... Time and again, I have found that the basic

evil behind today's ugliest phenomena is altruism. Well, I told you so. I have been telling you so since We The Living, which was published in 1936." Ayn Rand

Unfortunately, Rand's cynicism has permeated our political and social lives. You may choose between Ayn Rand's views of ethics as the pursuit of self-interest, or you can choose the virtue of the great religions: "*So whatever you wish that others would do to you, do also to them, for this is the Law and the Prophets."* (Mathew 7:12). Or, *"One should seek for others the happiness one desires for himself"* – Buddha. In Taoism - *"Regard your neighbor's gain as your gain, and your neighbor's loss as your own loss."*

Let me suggest an even more practical argument. From a Darwinian, survival of the fittest point of view, this teaching of altruism has survived through the ages in every great religion. Its universality and survival is a testimony to its truth and utility. The study of anthills and beehives has similarly demonstrated that service and sacrifice for the common good is an essential survival trait engrained in the genetic codes of bees and ants. It is engrained in our own as well.

Of course, Ayn Rand was an atheist who enjoyed the adoration (and book royalties!) of those seeking to justify their own pursuit of self-interest. But what every great religion taught as the Golden Rule is exactly what leads to a deeper and more authentic happiness. It turns out that doing for others, serving others, is ultimately in one's own self-interest, an investment returned in happiness.

Many authors write about the value of pursuing of a worthy purpose in life, a legacy upon which to look back. A worthy or noble purpose is never about oneself, but rather the good one may do for others. The knowledge that one is in pursuit of a noble purpose has the effect of ennobling oneself. One can argue that engaging in charity and service to others, sacrificing for others, is paradoxically, an act of self-interest because it leads to greater personal happiness.

Every organization has a responsibility to create a sense of meaning in the lives of those who dwell within its walls. Every great leader has understood his or her responsibility to ennoble their followers by holding up that which is worthy in their work and calling upon followers to sacrifice for that which is worthy, the good of the whole, the worthy purpose. In doing so, the leader is giving them the gift of self-worth and meaning.

5. Optimism and Creative Dissatisfaction Generate Performance

Norman Vincent Peal was right. *The Power of Positive Thinking* is one of the most popular management and self-help books of all time. He had no scientific data to support his philosophy, but like Dr. Deming, he had good intuition and powers of observation. You can summarize its guidance in this quote:

> *"Formulate and stamp indelibly on your mind a mental picture of yourself succeeding. Hold this picture tenaciously. Never permit it to fade. Your mind will seek to develop the picture...Do not build up obstacles in your imagination."*

Today we might view this as somewhat sophomoric advice from a bygone age. However, it turns out, that today's science proves that he was right on the money. Martin Seligman wrote a great book title *Learned Optimism* which followed his less happy book, *Learned Helplessness*. In it he cites a great deal of research that demonstrated that well-functioning, high performing, individuals are essentially optimistic and not pessimistic.

> *"The optimists and the pessimists: I have been studying them for the past twenty-five years. The defining characteristic of pessimists is that they tend to believe bad events will last a long time, will undermine everything they do, and are their own fault. The optimists, who are confronted with the same hard knocks of this world, think about misfortune in the opposite way. They tend to believe defeat is just a temporary setback, that its causes are confined to this one case. The optimists believe defeat is not their fault: Circumstances, bad luck, or other people brought it about. Such people are unfazed by defeat. Confronted by a bad situation, they perceive it as a challenge and try harder." Martin Seligman in Learned Optimism.*

In other words – hire optimists and not pessimists! Create a culture of optimism, of hope, of belief in a positive future for your organization. Winning cultures and winning teams are optimistic. No football coach before the game gave a speech to his team in which he said, "Well boys, we have no chance of beating this team, so let's go out there and take what's coming to us!" And, subsequently won the game. Losers tend to believe in their own defeat.

The positive psychology research has demonstrated that *"On average, optimistic individuals are healthier because they take care of themselves; optimistic students earn better grades because they go to class; optimistic insurance agents sell more policies because they make cold calls; and so on."* [14]

If you do these things, you will be applying much of the current research in positive psychology, and it will fulfill Dr. Deming's guidance to provide joy at work:

1. Build great teams! Be sure that every employee serves on a well-functioning team with knowledge of its purpose and its performance. Encourage celebration of winning team goals and setting records.
2. Build internal social networks around common interests and competencies. These learning networks provide both the joy of social relationships and the joy of learning.
3. Be sure to practice respect for people and recognize that the world's greatest experts are those who are on-the-spot, with their hands on the work. This builds their self-esteem and encourages learning.
4. Institute a process of gaining flexibility through multi-skilled, cross-trained employees who can optimize the effectiveness of their teams.
5. Stop wasting money where it does not pay off and spend it where it does. Pay employees for gaining skills and achieving performance. Value high performance by paying for it.
6. Know and promote the worthy purpose of your organization. Ennoble your employees by connecting them to a spirit of service. This is the essence of leadership.
7. Hire optimists and not pessimists. Generate hope and optimism by clearly stating where we are going and why it will be great when we get there. Generate creative dissatisfaction in yourself and your employees.

---

[14] Peterson, Christopher. Pursuing the Good Life. Oxford University Press, New York. 2013. P. 89.

Chapter 13

Google's Research on Team Performance

Google is one of the smartest companies on earth today. They pursue excellence in both their products and in their people. Some while ago they recognized that teams were the foundation of their organization and culture. Sound familiar? They have just completed a thorough research effort to determine what makes high performing teams at Google.

Fair Warning: I am biased. I particularly like this research because it exactly reinforces the need for the skills taught in my Team Leadership course. It is about the habits of interaction that produce a place of safety where team members can freely share, think together, and achieve a shared appreciation and consensus.

Let me summarize the key points with quotes from an article in the *New York Times Magazine.*[15]

The "Who" Part of the Equation Didn't Matter

In recent years there have been a number of personality tests created with the idea of selecting the right mix of personalities to form a team. This is generally a waste of time and money. How people behave and the practices of teams, far more than personalities, will determine the effectiveness of a team.

> *'We had lots of data, but there was nothing showing that a mix of specific personality types or skills or backgrounds made any difference. The "who" part of the equation didn't seem to matter.'*

---

[15] "What Google Learned From Its Quest to Build the Perfect Team" by Charles Duhigg, New York Times Magazine, February 25, 2016.

As the researchers studied the groups, however, they noticed two behaviors that all the good teams generally shared. First, on the good teams, members spoke in roughly the same proportion, a phenomenon the researchers referred to as "equality in distribution of conversational turn-taking." On some teams, everyone spoke during each task; on others, leadership shifted among teammates from assignment to assignment. But in each case, by the end of the day, everyone had spoken roughly the same amount. "As long as everyone got a chance to talk, the team did well," Woolley said. "But if only one person or a small group spoke all the time, the collective intelligence declined."

This finding points to the importance of facilitation skills on the part of the team leader. It is the primary function of a team leader, or facilitator, to make it easy for members to contribute, and to avoid dominance by a few members of the team. One of the tasks of a lean coach is to observe the behavior of team members, and the team leader and to provide helpful feedback. This is a key pattern of behavior that should be observed.

Second, the good teams all had high "average social sensitivity" — a fancy way of saying they were skilled at intuiting how others felt based on their tone of voice, their expressions and other nonverbal cues. One of the easiest ways to gauge social sensitivity is to show someone photos of people's eyes and ask him or her to describe what the people are thinking or feeling — an exam known as the Reading the Mind in the Eyes test. People on the more successful teams in Woolley's experiment scored above average on the Reading the Mind in the Eyes test. They seemed to know when someone was feeling upset or left out. People on the ineffective teams, in contrast, scored below average. They seemed, as a group, to have less sensitivity toward their colleagues.

The term *sensitivity* is not common in today's jargon of management. Many years ago there was a sensitivity training movement that followed the path too often followed to faddish excess. The excess killed it. However, the fundamental value of being sensitive to the emotions of others has not and never will lose its value. A great team leader, or team member, is sensitive to the emotional signals being sent by other members of the team.

Reject High Control and Order

Some team coaches are great believers in the importance of starting and ending on time, precisely following the agenda and the time allotted to each item, and eliminating or reducing "off-topic" conversation. But is that strict adherence to order characteristic of high performing teams? While there is value in each of those behaviors, there may be equal value in the social interactions that violate them.

> *Imagine you have been invited to join one of two groups.*
>
> *Team A is composed of people who are all exceptionally smart and successful. When you watch a video of this group working, you see professionals who wait until a topic arises in which they are expert, and then they speak at length, explaining what the group ought to do. When someone makes a side comment, the speaker stops, reminds everyone of the agenda and pushes the meeting back on track. This team is efficient. There is no idle chitchat or long debates. The meeting ends as scheduled and disbands so everyone can get back to their desks.*
>
> *Team B is different. It's evenly divided between successful executives and middle managers with few professional accomplishments. Teammates jump in and out of discussions. People interject and complete one another's thoughts. When a team member abruptly changes the topic, the rest of the group follows him off the agenda. At the end of the meeting, the meeting doesn't actually end: Everyone sits around to gossip and talk about their lives.*
>
> *The researchers eventually concluded that what distinguished the "good" teams from the dysfunctional groups was how teammates treated one another. The right norms, in other words, could raise a group's collective intelligence, whereas the wrong norms could hobble a team, even if, individually, all the members were exceptionally bright.*
>
> *But what was confusing was that not all the good teams appeared to behave in the same ways. "Some teams had a bunch of smart people who figured out how to break up work evenly," said Anita Woolley, the study's lead author. "Other groups had pretty average members, but they came up with ways to take advantage of everyone's relative*

strengths. Some groups had one strong leader. Others were more fluid, and everyone took a leadership role."

In other words, if you are given a choice between the serious-minded Team A or the free-flowing Team B, you should probably opt for Team B. Team A may be filled with smart people, all optimized for peak individual efficiency. But the group's norms discourage equal speaking; there are few exchanges of the kind of personal information that lets teammates pick up on what people are feeling or leaving unsaid. There's a good chance the members of Team A will continue to act like individuals once they come together, and there's little to suggest that, as a group, they will become more collectively intelligent.

In contrast, on Team B, people may speak over one another, go on tangents and socialize instead of remaining focused on the agenda. The team may seem inefficient to a casual observer. But all the team members speak as much as they need to. They are sensitive to one another's moods and share personal stories and emotions. While Team B might not contain as many individual stars, the sum will be greater than its parts.

Psychological Safety Leads to High Performance

When Google researchers encountered the concept of psychological safety in academic papers, it was as if everything suddenly fell into place. One engineer, for instance, had told researchers that his team leader was "direct and straightforward, which creates a safe space for you to take risks." That team, researchers estimated, was among Google's accomplished groups. By contrast, another engineer had told the researchers that his "team leader has poor emotional control." He added: "He panics over small issues and keeps trying to grab control. I would hate to be driving with him being in the passenger seat, because he would keep trying to grab the steering wheel and crash the car." That team, researchers presumed, did not perform well.

For Project Aristotle, research on psychological safety pointed to particular norms that are vital to success. There were other behaviors that seemed important as well — like making sure teams had clear goals and creating a culture of dependability. But Google's data indicated that psychological safety, more than anything else, was critical to making a team work.

What the Google researchers discovered from their own teams was common sense that they are now trying to make systematic.

The paradox, of course, is that Google's intense data collection and number crunching have led it to the same conclusions that good managers have always known. In the best teams, members listen to one another and show sensitivity to feelings and needs.

The fact that these insights aren't wholly original doesn't mean Google's contributions aren't valuable. In fact, in some ways, the "employee performance optimization" movement has given us a method for talking about our insecurities, fears and aspirations in more constructive ways. It also has given us the tools to quickly teach lessons that once took managers decades to absorb. Google, in other words, in its race to build the perfect team, has perhaps unintentionally demonstrated the usefulness of imperfection and done what Silicon Valley does best: figure out how to create psychological safety faster, better and in more productive ways.

The findings of this research should be an important input into the considerations of any coach. Are you looking for the behavior that indicates the desired sensitivity and caring for individuals that results in psychological safety? Many lean coaches come from engineering backgrounds and are very focused on measuring processes, scorecards, and eliminating waste. While all of those are valid concerns, they may at the same time miss the very soft indicators of effective teamwork.

Chapter 14

Case Study: VON Canada

Coaching & Lean Implementation Using A Blended Learning Model

By
Tracy Atkinson and Andrew Chan, VON Canada Lean Coaches
& Lawrence M. Miller

Summary

VON Canada, like many healthcare organizations, has been implementing lean management to reduce waste, improve customer service, productivity and financial performance. It has employed a combination of a) process redesign; b) online learning to provide team leaders with knowledge of lean practices; c) action-learning to develop new habits and skills; and d) internal coaching to assure continuous improvement. None of these elements alone would have been successful; however, the blended combination of these elements has produced significant improvements in performance.

VON has reported a very significant change in their culture, as well as increases in productivity of between 25% and 37% varying by district. These changes also resulted in reductions in downtime, reduced overtime and travel expenses.

VON referred to their new lean culture as the "VON Way." The "VON Way" has changed the way VON engages staff members and provides services to clients. VON service delivery team members are now engaged in greater self-management and continuous improvement. The "VON Way" has created a new social system and a strong team culture.

Background

VON Canada (formerly Victorian Order of Nurses) is a charitable organization which has been providing home and community care services since 1897. These services include Nursing, Home Support Services, a variety of clinics and community support programs. VON employs approximately five thousand care providers, and approximately 250 management and line staff. Home care delivery is funded by the Canadian government through a network of local Community Care Access Centres (CCAC).

Until recently, VON was the sole provider for home health care in Nova Scotia with little concern about competition. This changed recently. Over the past decade VON has faced increasing financial pressures, competition, a declining health care workforce and rising client demands.

While all of VON Canada's Districts have followed a similar model, this case study focuses on one District in the eastern province of Nova Scotia with two sites - Cape Breton and Antigonish. These sites employ two hundred Nurses, the Site Management team (four Nurse Managers and a District Executive Director), schedulers, and an administrative staff. On average the two sites have been providing over 23,000 homecare visits per month.

The Condition Prior to Lean Implementation

A major factor in the productivity of home care service is how nurses and home support workers are scheduled. This determines the efficiency of travel times and the number of visits a service provider makes per day. This in turn determines financial results.

Prior to lean implementation, the scheduling process was centralized, and situated five hours away from the two sites. It was cumbersome, and there was no accountability on the part of those doing the scheduling, since there was no visibility of scheduler's work. The structure did not support team work. There was a wall, a siloed structure, separating the work of those who scheduled home visits and those who provided the service. This resulted in a culture of blaming and denial of responsibility. The cost of service delivery was high due to too many steps in the scheduling process. For example, the data entry of clients and the scheduling of these clients were completed by two different people. This resulted in high unscheduled time 10% to 20%, and waste of 10% to 20% of nurse's time during which they were not visiting clients. High overtime of 10%, high travel time and distance were regular occurrences which added to the inefficiencies. This also led to delay accepting new clients.

There was little discussion about performance measures or targets during staff meetings. When there was a new target introduced, site management would meet with the Nurses to advise them of the new goals; however, the site management team was not involved in the creation of these goals. Neither the site management team, nor the nurses, felt ownership for the goals.

The site management teams were in a "fire-fighting mode." There was no disciplined problem-solving. When the site management attempted to make improvements, they were difficult to implement and changes were short lived.

VON's structure and culture were resistant to change. The Cape Breton and Antigonish sites had high retention rates since Nurses were used to following their own preferences. The site managers had minimal control over the scheduling practices and felt helpless to improve any of the core work processes.

Lean Redesign: Changing the System

VON Canada made a commitment to lean management principles, and began by following the consultant's *Whole-System Redesign* model.[16] This involved local design teams re-mapping their work flow to eliminate waste, and speed cycle times. It also involved designing a team structure to move toward increasing self-management as teams took responsibility for their own performance. In Spring of 2015, Cape Breton and Antigonish had redesigned their client service delivery system to include the following:

1. All employees will experience a change in the way they work. It was necessary to involve everyone, service providers and managers in the assumption that *we are all in this together and we all must change.* While the principles of redesign were common to the larger organization, it was important that the local design team included both managers and service providers at the local level. This gave them ownership and enabled implementation.

---

[16] See *Getting to Lean – Transformational Change Management* by Lawrence M. Miller.

2. The entire work-flow, from the time the local referral agency contacted the VON office with a need for service, to the completed service and billing, was completely remapped to eliminate waste in the form of unnecessary steps, delays and hand-offs. Approximately 50% of the steps in the original process were eliminated.
3. Silos, walls between functions, were eliminated by introducing a new scheduling role within the local site called the Client Service Associate (CSA).
4. The CSA were co-located with the sites they support, and now play a key role in supporting service delivery teams. This allows for team work to occur. Both service providers and the CSA are now on the same team, reporting to the same manager, and responsible for the same results.

CHANGING HABITS

VON leadership recognized that changing the system alone would not result in a sustainable change in long established habits. This would require a learning model that could be applied over an extended period of time. To accomplish this they adopted a *blended learning model* of self-paced online instruction, action-learning to practice and apply the new skills, and one-on-one coaching to encourage and reinforce the adoption of the new skills.

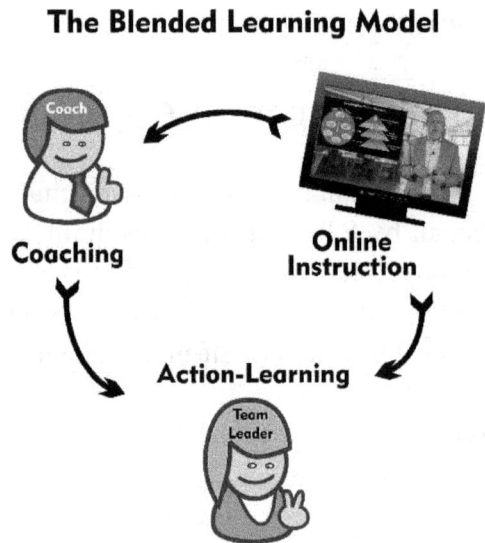

The Blended Learning Model

SELF-PACED ONLINE LEARNING

VON leadership recognized that all managers, who would now become team leaders, would need to receive training in team leadership, problem-solving, and the principles of lean management. Because VON Canada has sites spread over all of the Central and Eastern Provinces of Canada, and very little money to devote to training, the ability to bring people together for training in the traditional workshop method was not possible. The external consultant developed an online course (*Team Leadership* – aka, *Team Kata*) with seventy-one lectures covering the topics of lean principles, team formation, problem-solving, process improvement, communication and facilitation.

The curriculum of this course included the following sections and topics:

4. **Organizing Your Team**
    a. Developing a Team Charter.
    b. Clarifying roles and responsibilities.
    c. Developing a Team Agenda.
    d. Developing a Team Scorecard and Display
5. **Solving Problems and Improving Performance**
    a. Root Cause Analysis
    b. Brainstorming
    c. Plan-Do-Check (or Study)- Act Problem-solving.
    d. Action Planning
    e. The A3 Problem-solving Process
    f. Mapping Your Value Stream and Eliminating Waste
    g. Improving Motivation and Human Performance Problems
    h. Developing Standard Work and Leader Standard Work
6. **Personal Effectiveness Skills**
    a. Team Facilitation Skills
    b. Effective Listening
    c. Giving and Receiving Feedback

VON leadership also formed a small cadre of internal coaches who would meet with teams after they had viewed a section of the course to assist the teams in applying the lessons to their situation. This began to encourage Site Management to change their approach to problem-solving by using the lean problem-solving models of Plan-Do-Study-Act and the more comprehensive A3 model. .

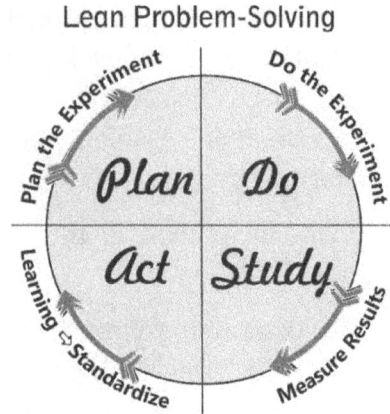

Although the site management was challenged with demanding day-to-day tasks, the site embraced the training from the beginning and made it part of their daily routine. Site management would often complete the *Team Leadership* course on their own time. They could do this at home, on a tablet, or their work computer. Some used the Udemy app on the cell phone to listen to the lectures as they drove in their car.

The online *Team Leadership* course made acquiring the knowledge of lean practices relatively easy. However, we wanted more than knowledge – we wanted action and results!

ACTION-LEARNING

We learn with all of our senses and at VON Canada we realized that we had to employ all of these senses in the learning process. Blended learning assumes that no one mode of learning will result in the adoption of new patterns of thought or behavior. It assumes a *learning system* that employs multiple forms of learning over an extended period of time.

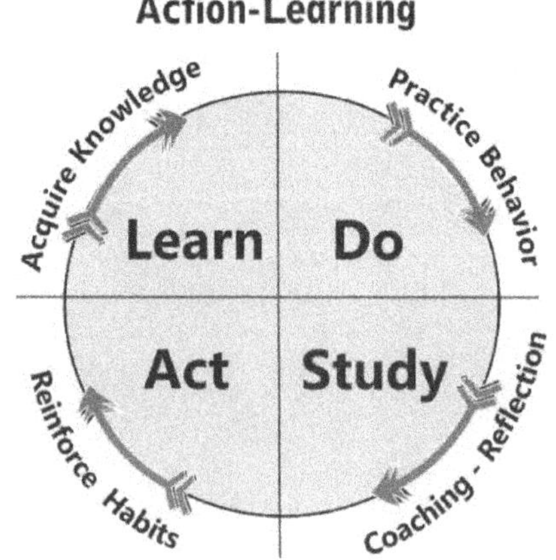

The *action-learning* process at VON involved demonstrating new skills by every leader along with his or her team. It is very much like the PDSA problem-solving model in that it is a cycle of learning through experimentation.

The more critical stage of learning - and this is where coaching was most helpful, is when the Nurse Managers and Team Leaders practiced the new behavior and received feedback and encouragement. They learned and then practiced their new skills with their team. For example, the team practiced problem-solving skills, led by their team leader. They went through a sequence of continuous improvement steps, repeating the Plan-Do-Study-Act cycle, developing their skills each time. The Team Leader gave feedback to the team and the Coach gave feedback to the Team Leader.

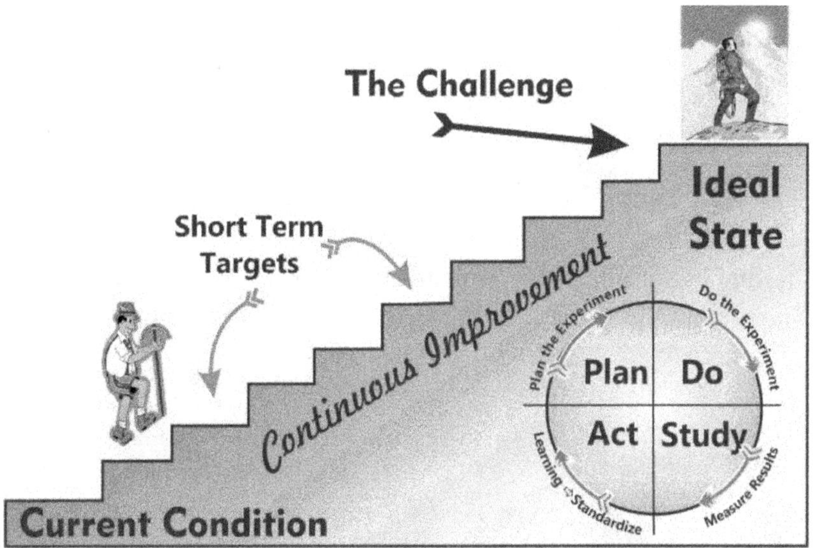

Lean management, which is derived from the Toyota Production System, is founded on the very simple idea of continuous improvement. Rather than assuming that there is one right way, it assumes a continuous process of learning through experimentation. There is always a current state of performance; a desired target for improvement; and an ideal state which can never be completely achieved. There is an acceptance of the experimentation, or trial-and-error improvement. This acceptance of experimentation reduces the fear of failure and promotes an understanding that we can always strive for a better way. Establishing this mindset has been a major accomplishment of the lean effort at VON Canada.

COACHING

In order to sustain the changes in behavior VON recognized the need to develop competent internal coaches. To continue to provide quality service to their clients VON established the Lean Centre of Excellence with 4 Lean Coaches (2 in Nova Scotia and 2 in Ontario) and a Director. The Lean Centre of Excellence supported the development of the "VON Way" by adopting lean methodology.

The important element is that VON is striving to provide every manager with a coach. This is the practice at Toyota and VON adopted the same model. This can only be accomplished by adopting a peer-to-peer coaching model supported by the more experienced fulltime coaches.

The learning and coaching process was facilitated by the fact that every level of management, including the Senior Management Team, was participating in the same training and coaching. Senior managers could then model behavior, and reinforce that behavior at the next level.

Team Coaches at VON Canada

The online course is accompanied by a Coaching Map. This map defines the sections of the course, the action steps the leader and team should take based on that lesson, and coaching questions the coach should ask the leader or team. Because the course is very comprehensive, the author was asked to identify the "critical few" lessons and actions on which the teams should focus. These critical steps included defining the team charter, their scorecard, creating visual display, and mapping their process. The additional sections of the course are important skills for leaders, communication and facilitation skills, etc., but not the most essential for improving performance in the short term. This map became the focus for both coaches and teams.

While Site Management continued with the online course, the new service delivery system went live in Nova Scotia in July 2015.

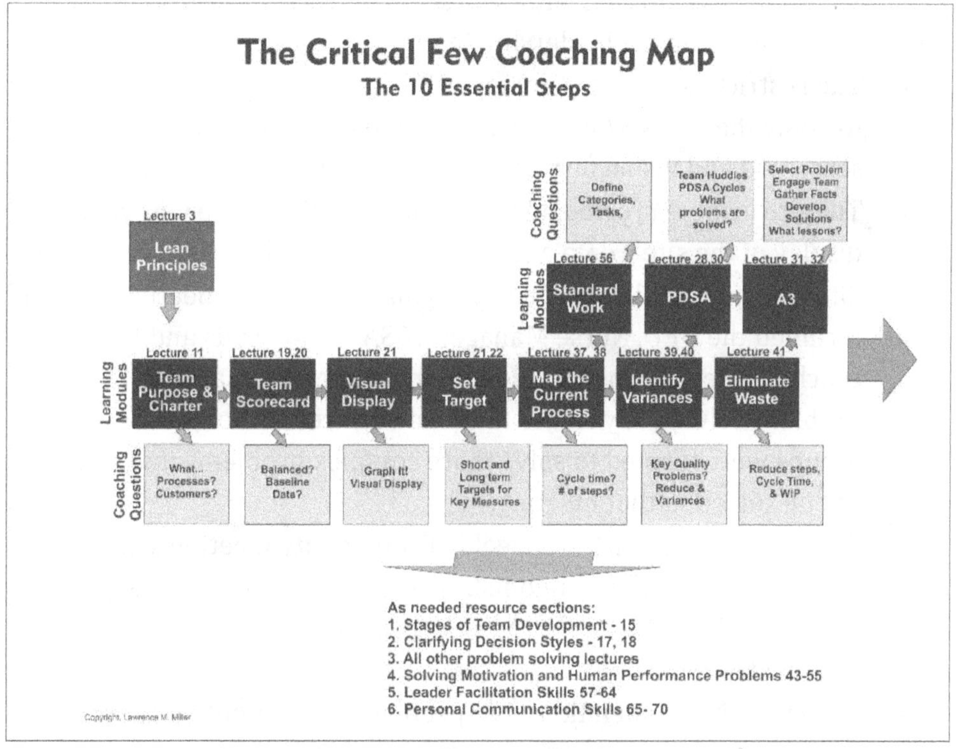

IMPLEMENTATION

The Site Management team and the redesign project team had daily meetings after the implementation of the redesigned process and captured all problems on an issue log. The Site leadership team, along with Project team, conducted root cause analysis to determine how to resolve the issues. At first, Site managers wanted to quickly jump to the solution prior to understanding the problem. This was the old cultural habits. The lean coach got them to state the problem, the impact, and by asking them the “five why's" to determine the root of the issue. Once these items were completed, the team worked on a possible solution. By Sept 2015, all forty issues that had been logged were solved, and there was an action plan for each.

Site Management and lean coaches began coaching Nurses on the new processes and the new device technology, and coaching Client Service Associates on enhancing their scheduling practices.

In the fall of 2015 the following changes had been implemented:

- With the support of the lean coach, the site management team developed a team charter, a scorecard and standard work for all levels including the leadership team.
- The District Executive Director (DED) coached the Nurse Managers to apply the "VON Way" which included team problem-solving, a scorecard and visual display, and recognition for improvements.
- The site leaders created a LEAN room in which there was visual display of the site's data and illustration of the latest process maps.
- Site leaders established weekly regular leadership meetings which included the DED, Nurse Managers, CSA Team Leads and Lean coach. These meetings included review of performance data and problem-solving any issues that had surfaced. In some cases, sub-groups were formed to solve more complex problems that could not be solved in that meeting.
- Site leaders also started a weekly Productivity meeting separately for Cape Breton and Antigonish. These included the Nurse Managers, DED, Nurses, CSAs, CSA Team Leads, and Site Administrators.
- In all meetings, when there is a problem that cannot be solved quickly, the A3 format, which is taught in the *Team Leadership* course is used.

The District Executive Director made the online *Team Leadership* course a priority to her site management team. She also "modeled the VON Way" by going to the Gemba (where the work gets done), visiting the CSA room regularly to ask questions and learn from their own problem-solving.

Using positive reinforcement to develop the new habits of teamwork was encouraged by the lean coaches. This included encouraging the District Executive Director to follow-up with the Customer Service Associates

(CSAs), who do the scheduling, when there was a new productivity improvement. This both provided encouragement and reinforced following the new standard work that had been defined. Previously, there was little in the way of personal relationship between the DED or site leaders and those who did the scheduling. Now, a personal caring relationship was being created that enabled the managers to provide more direct coaching to both the CSAs and the service providers.

RESULTS:

All of the important indicators of performance improved significantly. It is impossible to separate the results caused by the redesigned process versus the results of training and coaching. The improved measures included the key productivity measure of weekly home visits per nurse, a significant reduction in over-time hours and a reduction of travel expenses.

- The most critical measure that impacted productivity was visits per full-time nurse equivalent (FTEs). It increased from approximately 36 per week to 43 per week in the district highlighted in this case study. Throughout the larger organization, on average, visits increased from 35 to 48 visits per FTE, or 37% employing the same blended learning model.
- Over-time decreased from 10% of total hours to under 1%,
- Unscheduled time, a clear form of waste, decreased from 10 to 20% to below 2% of total time.

There have been many changes in the social system and behavior. One obvious example of this is the daily huddles, a brief team meeting of local nurse teams. In these huddles the nurses and CSAs review any scheduling problems, and solve them on-the-spot. Despite the fact that the nurses are in the field and huddling virtually, there is an 80% attendance rate at the daily huddles.

The Site experienced some turnover with Nurses due to the culture change. Under the new system, there is visibility to everyone's work which made everyone more accountable. The majority of the nurses enjoyed the new streamlined processes and team environment

VON leadership felt that some form of recognition for completing the Team Leadership course, and implementing all of the required action steps, deserved some positive reinforcement. Rather than rely on external

Nurse Managers Laurie Clark, Frances Magliaro, and District Manager Elizabeth MacDonald with their Yellow Belt Award

certification, they created their own Yellow Belt award. In May 2015, the site management team had started the Team Leadership course and they completed this in the winter of 2015. They received their Yellow Belt award presented to them in person by VON's CEO, Jo-Anne Poirier.

Chapter 15

Case Study: The Honda Way

I wrote the following case study in 1989. Many of the details may be out of date. However, the important lessons of building and aligning a culture will never be out of date.

As you read this you may wish to consider your own culture and how it has been designed to maximize human performance, quality and customer satisfaction. The following graphic is one way to describe the influences, internal and external, on the culture of any organization. I organized my observations as I visited Honda's plant according to this model.

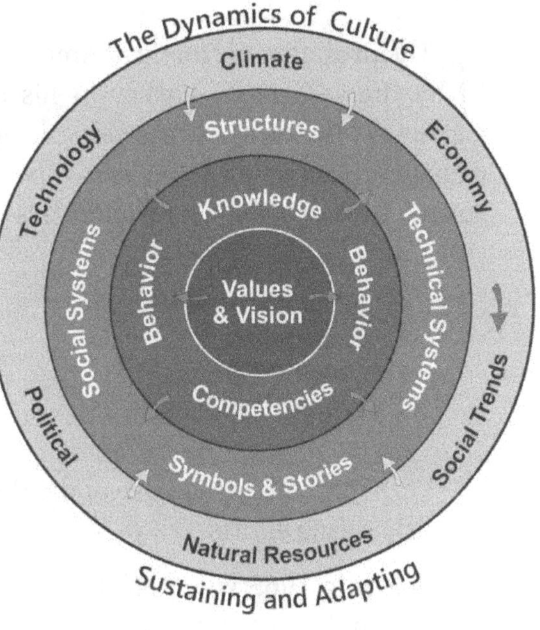

During the early days of Honda America Manufacturing's operations in Marysville, Ohio, they used my book *American Spirit* as a management development text. This resulted in several invitations to visit and present to the Honda management group and supplier groups. I wrote the following after my first two-day visit to the Marysville plants.

I spent two days touring the plants, speaking with managers and production associates, sitting in on meetings, and asking lots of questions. Why is Honda so good? The answer is both simple and complex. It is a combination of technical, or work process design; and, their unique culture.

There is nothing that stands out as their single secret to quality. The secret is - they do everything - and they do it as a team!

I find that in every healthy corporate culture there is a common understanding of philosophy, the values and visions upon which decisions and practices are based. The management practices, the structure, systems, skills, style, and symbols are consistent with the philosophy. At Honda there is clearly a "Team" culture.

Even before entering the building, the philosophy became evident. As we drove toward the plant I noticed lines of newly planted trees. I was told that they were planted by newly hired associates. Each new associate plants a tree "so they can grow with the company." All associates (the term used for all employees) know the company philosophy. They see it every day in a hundred ways. They hear it consistently from their leaders. There are no contradictions.

The president of Honda of America is Shoichiro Irimajiri, known as Mr. Iri by the associates. Earlier in his career, Mr. Iri was responsible for managing Honda's successful racing efforts, designing engines and managing production facilities in Japan. He frequently speaks of the "Racing Spirit." The Racing Spirit includes five principles:

1. ***Seek the challenger.***
2. ***Be ready on time.***
3. ***Teamwork.***
4. ***Quick Response.***
5. ***Winner Takes All!***

Perhaps more instructive of the Honda philosophy is his story of one of his early racing efforts.

It was in 1965 when Mr. Iri was working on the Formula One racing engines. In the British Grand Prix of that year, the engine failed and it was torn down and examined by Mr. Honda himself.

Examining the failed piston, he turned to Shoichiro Irimajiri and demanded, "Who designed this piston?" "I did," he acknowledged. After examining the engineering drawing Mr. Honda roared out, 'You! Stupid! No wonder the piston gets burned. You have changed the thickness here."

After the young Irimajiri attempted to defend his design change with some data from previous engines, Mr. Honda roared again: "I hate college graduates! They use only their heads. Do you really think you can use such obsolete data obtained from old, low-performance engines? I have been making and designing pistons for several years. I am fully aware how critical half a millimeter is here. A company does not need people like you who use only their heads. Before you laid out this design, why didn't you listen to opinions of those experienced people in the shop? If you think academic study in college is everything, you are totally wrong. You will be useless in Honda unless you spend more time on-the-spot for many years to come."

"You will go to the machining shop," Mr. Honda ordered the young engineer, "and you will apologize to every person there, for you have wasted their efforts." Mr. Honda followed him down the hall to make sure he did as directed. Mr. Iri recalls that he was only glad that he had no ambition of becoming president of the company. He was not even sure he would succeed as an engineer. He learned his lesson. He not only succeeded as an engineer, designing several successful racing engines, but he became the president of Honda of America, the first Japanese company to export cars back to Japan. Shoichiro Irimajiri still listens to those experienced people in the shop and he is not wasting their time.

The Honda philosophy stresses to be on-the-spot in the plant and see the problem, touch the part, and gain experience in the actual job, in order to effectively solve a problem.[17] Engineers and management spend most of their time in the factory, in touch with their associates, the product, and the process. The Honda philosophy is manifested in all of the management practices. In the symbols, structure, systems, skills, and style [18], the philosophy can be seen and experienced every day, by every employee, every hour.

SYMBOLS:

When I arrived at the Marysville plant I was given a uniform to wear in the plant. I was told that this wasn't given to all guests, only "honored guests." To cover my tie with the white smock with the Honda name, to look the same as every other associate, was an honor. I can assure you that by the time my visit was finished it felt like an honor. To be part of a proud group of people, to share their symbol of equality, caused me to feel a part, invested, in their shared goals.

---

[17] In recent years this has become known as the "Gemba" walk.

[18] These five "S's" have been used by myself and others as a structure of organization design, or "socio-technical systems" design.

All associates, from president to newest hired associate, eat in the same cafeteria, park in the same undesignated parking spaces, and managers sit at the same metal desks in open office areas. Most of the desks are arranged in blocks of six, often with paired Japanese and American managers sitting across from one another. All of the managers of the motorcycle plant sit at one block of six identical desks, the Japanese vice-president and the American plant manager sitting across from each other.

As I walked through the plant, the cleanest non-food manufacturing plant out of several hundred I have been in, I observed a vice-president stop and pick up a misplaced object on the floor. There is nothing on the floor. There are also no maintenance people to clean up! Everyone, every associate and manager, cleans his or her own work area.

To many, these symbols will seem trivial. They would be if they stood alone, at odds with the behavior and attitudes of the people, or if the structure and systems stood in contradiction. However, they are one part of a total system, like a well-engineered engine with all components balanced and moving in unison. Symbols, structure, systems, skills and style are all aligned.

STRUCTURE:

Everyone is a member of a team. The team is the first level of organization. At the beginning of a shift every associate meets with his team and team leader. The day's work is discussed and feedback on the previous day's quality is given. Any problems, changes, or concerns are shared during this meeting.

A team is comprised of 15 to 20 associates who work in a common area. As I toured both the auto and motorcycle plant, I stood and watched the assembly line in operation. I asked which person was the team leader and which was the production coordinator, the second-level manager. It was very hard to find them or distinguish them. I watched as there was an apparent problem on the motorcycle line.

One employee, having difficulty getting a frame over an engine assembly, had stopped the line. He and another associate worked frantically to get the frame in place. It took about twenty seconds for the line to move again. I asked where the team leader was. The other associate, helping to form the frame, was the team leader. The production coordinator was at the next station on the assembly line helping another associate catch up on the placement of electrical wire assemblies. I watched for about fifteen minutes as the team leader and production coordinator (equivalent of first-line supervisor and department manager) worked on the line, smiling, joking, and working hard and fast with their associates.

Nowhere is there a private office for team leaders or production coordinators. They do not remove themselves from the work. They are on-the-spot, seeing and touching the product, gaining experience and solving problems. They are part of the working team.

All managers are organized into teams and solve problems together. The structure of the organization, as well as the physical arrangement of desks and offices, makes group problem-solving a natural and constant occurrence.

Participation in the continuous improvement process is also structured through Quality Circles. NH Circles (NH stands for "Now Honda, New Honda, Next Honda") are similar to quality circles in many other companies. However, at Honda they are one component of a total involvement process which they call of VIP (Voluntary Involvement Program).

VIP includes a suggestion system, quality awards, and safety awards. Twenty percent of all associates participate in circles. The rate of suggestion adoption is 59.4 percent, and 60 percent participate in some component of the VIP process. In speaking with several NH Circle members, I was impressed that they felt the responsibility to see that accepted recommendations for improvement were implemented. They also felt that their circles were different from those in other companies in that they are constantly looking for any improvement in the production process, large or small, and even small improvements are highly valued. They said that the success of Honda was the result of constantly finding small improvements, not just looking for major ones.

System:

I expected to find systems of employee involvement at Marysville. However, I was somewhat surprised to see the amount of thought put into the positive reinforcement systems. Honda of America practices performance management, or as I used to call it "behavior management." They have found ways to provide constant feedback, recognition, and tangible positive reinforcement for almost every form of desirable performance.

The NH Circle program, suggestion system, quality awards, and safety awards are all tied together with a point system. Every associate earns points by participating in any of these improvement processes. Awards include award certificates, gift certificates, Department Manager's Award, Plant Manager's Award, and President's Award. These also result in points accumulating over your career, and these points can earn a Honda Civic (that's for 2,500 points) and an Accord (5,000 points), plus two weeks off with pay and airplane tickets to anywhere in the world with spending money.

In addition to hourly or salaried compensation, all associates participate in profit sharing. This profit sharing is an innovation of Honda of America and is not part of the system in Japan. Ten percent of the gross profit generated by Honda Motor Company is shared with associates based on their relative compensation. Good attendance results in another bonus. The average bonus check for attendance in 1986 was $832. The average profit sharing check was $2,688.

Performance analysis and feedback is an important part of any total performance management system. In each of the open office areas and in each of the many conference rooms, all of the walls are literally covered with charts and graphs representing different quality and productivity performance variables. The graphs are of every possible variety, some employing Statistical Process Control methods and some simply reflecting historical data with means, trends, and goal lines. Frequently, along with the charts on the wall are lists of causes or solutions to problems. Diagrams of auto parts or production machinery with arrows pointing to sources of problems are also frequent. It is obvious that all of the managers at Honda are in touch with plant performance data.

Another system worthy of mention is the discipline system. There are some fairly traditional and sound procedures for gradual counseling and discipline. However, the unique part of the discipline process is the peer review provided for associates who are dismissed for poor conduct. If an associate wishes to appeal a termination, a peer review panel is formed by randomly selecting six or eight production associates. One senior manager also serves on the panel with equal vote. The panel hears both sides of the case and then decides to overturn or accept the management decision. Nine out of ten times the decisions are upheld by the associates.

Skills:

The measure of skills is found in the work product. There is no question Honda has highly skilled engineering and quality personnel. Most engineers are Japanese. Hiring and training more Americans is a goal for coming years. Honda is an engineering company. Most of the Japanese senior managers have served as design engineers for engines, including racing engines, or other components.

Having worked at other auto companies, it soon became obvious to me that at Honda the most valued personnel are those with engineering and technical competence. At many other companies, it is the financial managers and management professionals who are most valued. Honda is in the business of making excellent cars. Many other companies are in the business of making money, and, only secondarily, making cars. Honda makes money and does not need layers of bureaucratic managers because they are passionately dedicated to their technology and products.

On the assembly line, there is a process of continual skill development. Associates are rotated from one position to another to broaden their skills and increase their flexibility. Even when applicants are interviewed for employment at Honda, they are asked questions to determine their flexibility. Flexibility and the development of broad-based skills is a central principle.

At Honda, it is assumed the production associates are intelligent, skilled, and dedicated. They can, therefore, be trusted to manage the quality process. Every associate is a quality control inspector. The assembly process at Honda is based on just-in-time (JIT) inventory and assumption of 100 percent quality parts. Each associate knows it is his or her job to inspect each part to assure conformance to requirements. Any associate can reject a part. If a manager wants the part used after the associate has rejected it, the burden is on the manager to explain to the associate why it should be used. There is a quality assurance department with a team of associates who will call the suppliers regarding any and every bad part. Every vendor is assigned to one associate, who knows exactly who to call, including home telephones, to provide immediate feedback on any deviation from quality requirements.

STYLE:

All of the methods described above are held together by people with a sense of humor and a high level of people-to-people skills.

As I interviewed managers, I repeatedly asked them how they felt working for, or with, Japanese managers. I wanted to know if there was any resentment toward the Japanese. I could find absolutely none. I could only find the sincerest respect and friendship. There was no feeling of "us Americans" working for "them." The reason for this mutual respect became clear the next morning.

Every morning the 10 or 12 managers of the motorcycle plant meet to review performance, solve problems, and make plans for the day. The Japanese vice-president responsible for the motorcycle operations sat at the end of the table. The meeting was led by a manager who was two levels down. There was a lively discussion about the handling of an "almost-in-time" inventory situation that had almost halted production the previous day. There were three or four Japanese managers and about eight Americans in the meeting. One of the Japanese managers was very vocal about how confusing the situation was and how it should have been handled better. Several others discussed what happened and how it was being resolved today. The vice-president sat quietly through a half hour of discussion, never saying anything until the meeting was coming to a conclusion. Only then did he speak out. He had two points. First, he wanted to thank everyone for their efforts yesterday, rising to meet the challenge presented by their problem. Second, he wanted to stress how important it was to meet another challenge that was coming up within the next week. His tone was calm and reassuring.

These incidents, and dozens of others like them, proved to me that the integration of cultures is working in Marysville. The Americans have adopted the Japanese patience and view things from a long-term perspective. The Japanese have adopted, or at least accepted, the American fun-loving familiarity and creativity.

The style at Honda is different than at other Japanese companies and this may be central to their success and initiative in manufacturing in the United States. The traditional Japanese company places a high value on age and seniority. Honda does not. Mr. Irimajiri is a young man excited by winning races and building racing engines. Mr. Honda has retired because he believes the company should be run by young men. The first principle of Honda management policy is: "Proceed always with ambition and youthfulness." The second is: "Respect sound theory, develop fresh ideas and make the most effective use of time." The third is: "Enjoy your work, and always brighten your working atmosphere."

Honda now employs 6,000 youthful-minded and creative Buckeye associates in Marysville

. That number will be raised to over 8,000 as the second auto assembly plant is built nearby.[19] The U.S.-manufactured content of the Honda Accord is now about 60 percent and will be increased to 75 percent. The Accord is more American than some GM, Ford, or Chrysler nameplates with higher imported content.

As I left Marysville, I didn't leave with the feeling that I had visited a "foreign" manufacturer. Rather, I had the feeling that I had visited something new. I had visited a world-embracing company, with a world-embracing philosophy, as much American as Japanese, perhaps the best of both world. I could also think of nothing that Honda was doing, no secret in either principle or practice, which could not be adopted by any company - if its senior managers were knowledgeable, committed, and would "proceed always with youthfulness."

---

[19] That number is now close to twelve thousand employees.

PART THREE

EXERCISES AND TOOLS

A. **COACHING WORKSHEET**

B. **ACTION PLAN**

C. **DAILY LEADERSHIP BEHAVIOR – LEADING WITH RESPECT**

D. **COACHING MAPS**

E. **TEAM MEETING OBSERVATIONS**

F. **IMPROVING TEAM DYNAMICS**

G. **HOW FAR ALONG THE LEAN JOURNEY ARE WE?**

Coaching Worksheet	
Who are you coaching?	
What is the Desired Skill?	
What is your positive assumption?	
List component pinpointed behaviors of this skill:	
What is the current condition and how do you know this?	
How will you model the behavior?	

When, where, and with whom will you practice the behavior and skill?	
Provide coaching. How did it work? What did you learn?	
How did you reinforce improvement (shape behavior)?	
Did behavior change?	
Did feelings change?	
How would you do a better job of coaching in the future?	

Action Plan			
Team:			
Problem:			
Counter Measure:			
Action – What?	**Who Will Act?**	**When?**	**Status**

Team
Kata

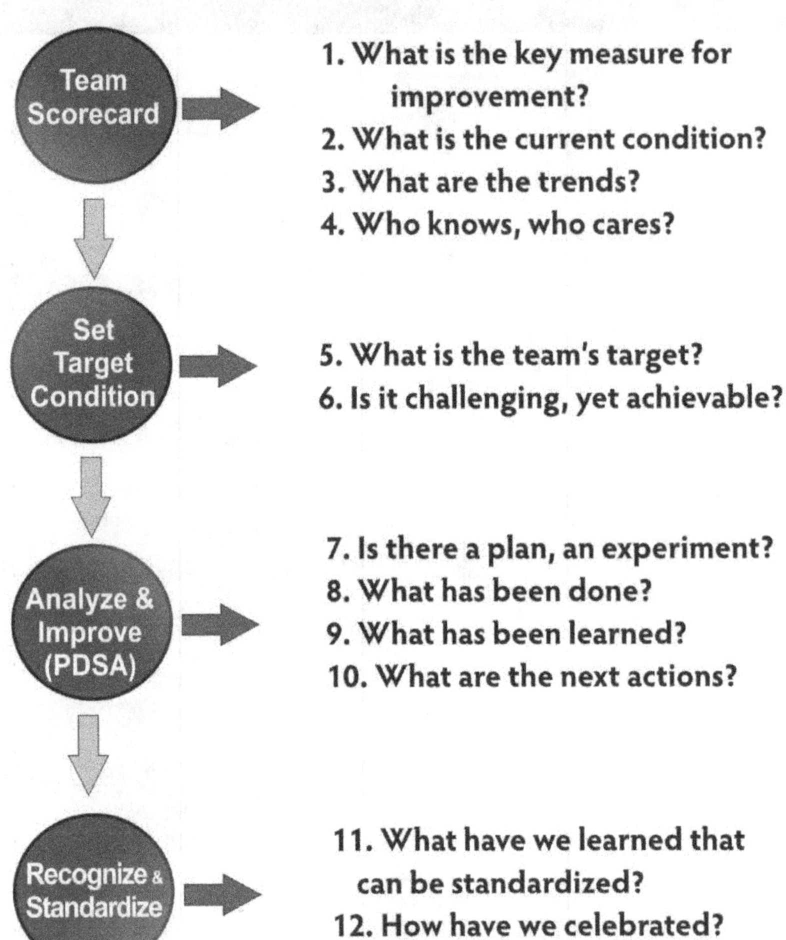
Leading With Respect
Questions to Engage and Empower
Team Scorecard
1. What is the key measure for improvement?
2. What is the current condition?
3. What are the trends?
4. Who knows, who cares?
Set Target Condition
5. What is the team's target?
6. Is it challenging, yet achievable?
Analyze & Improve (PDSA)
7. Is there a plan, an experiment?
8. What has been done?
9. What has been learned?
10. What are the next actions?
Recognize & Standardize
11. What have we learned that can be standardized?
12. How have we celebrated?
Daily Leadership Behavior

Coaching Maps

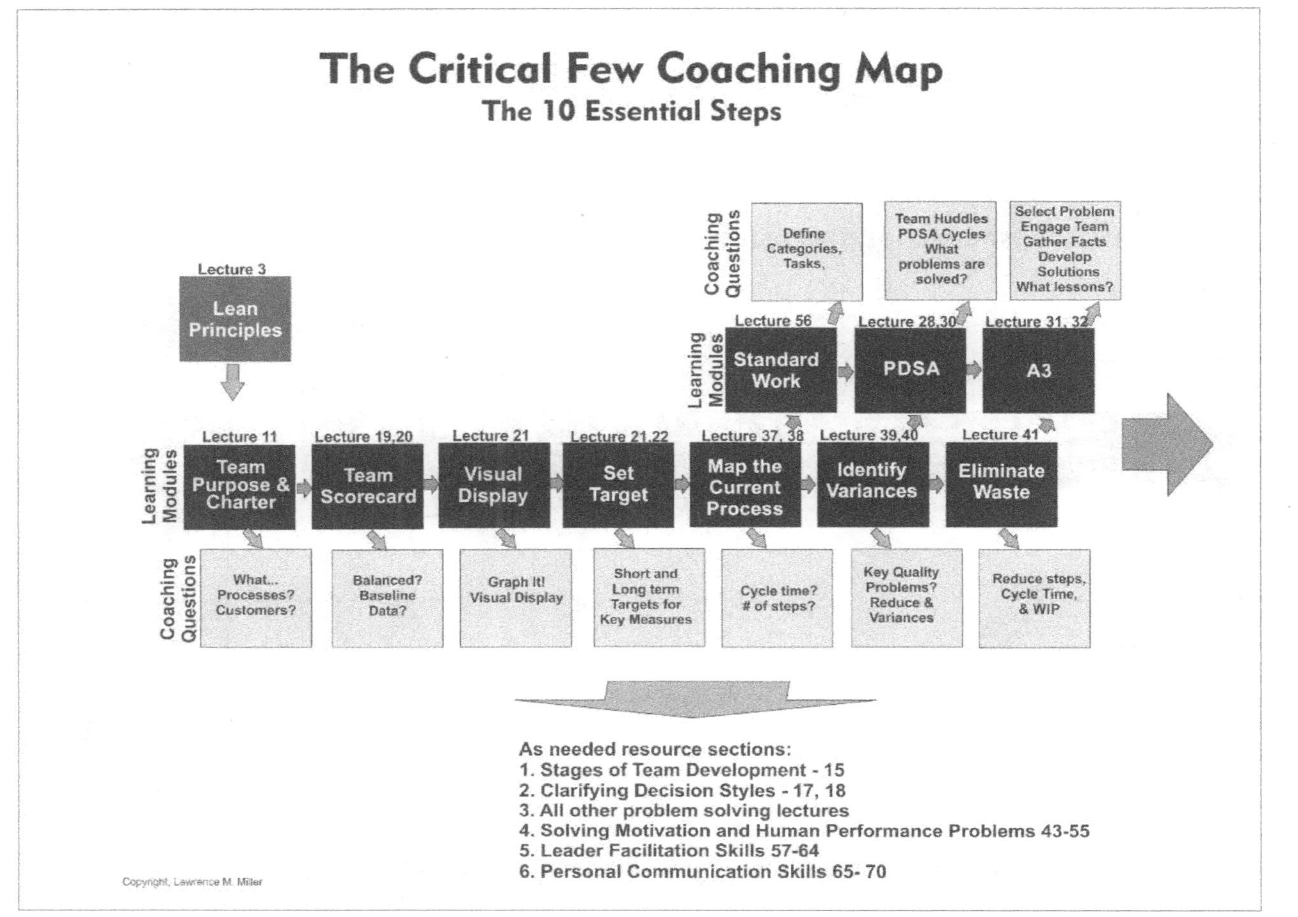

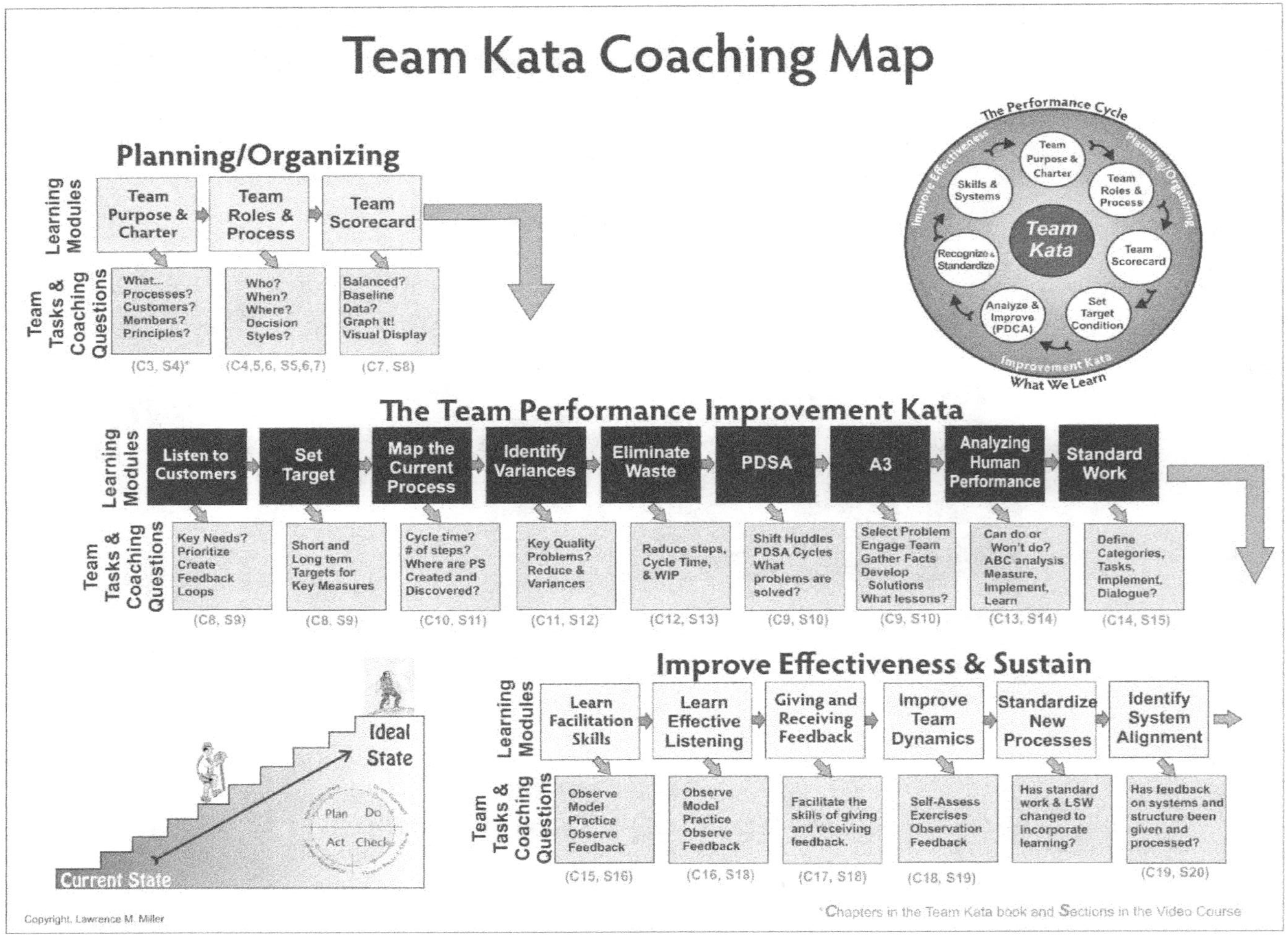
Team Kata Coaching Map
Planning/Organizing
Learning Modules
Team Tasks & Coaching Questions
Team Purpose & Charter
Team Roles & Process
Team Scorecard
What... Processes? Customers? Members? Principles?
Who? When? Where? Decision Styles?
Balanced? Baseline Data? Graph It! Visual Display
(C3, S4)*
(C4,5,6, S5,6,7)
(C7, S8)
The Performance Cycle
Planning/Organizing
Improvement Kata
What We Learn
Improve Effectiveness
Team Kata
Team Purpose & Charter
Team Roles & Process
Team Scorecard
Set Target Condition
Analyze & Improve (PDCA)
Recognize & Standardize
Skills & Systems
The Team Performance Improvement Kata
Listen to Customers
Set Target
Map the Current Process
Identify Variances
Eliminate Waste
PDSA
A3
Analyzing Human Performance
Standard Work
Key Needs? Prioritize Create Feedback Loops
Short and Long term Targets for Key Measures
Cycle time? # of steps? Where are PS Created and Discovered?
Key Quality Problems? Reduce & Variances
Reduce steps, Cycle Time, & WIP
Shift Huddles PDSA Cycles What problems are solved?
Select Problem Engage Team Gather Facts Develop Solutions What lessons?
Can do or Won't do? ABC analysis Measure, Implement, Learn
Define Categories, Tasks, Implement, Dialogue?
(C8, S9)
(C8, S9)
(C10, S11)
(C11, S12)
(C12, S13)
(C9, S10)
(C9, S10)
(C13, S14)
(C14, S15)
Improve Effectiveness & Sustain
Current State
Ideal State
Plan
Do
Act
Check
Learn Facilitation Skills
Learn Effective Listening
Giving and Receiving Feedback
Improve Team Dynamics
Standardize New Processes
Identify System Alignment
Observe Model Practice Observe Feedback
Observe Model Practice Observe Feedback
Facilitate the skills of giving and receiving feedback.
Self-Assess Exercises Observation Feedback
Has standard work & LSW changed to incorporate learning?
Has feedback on systems and structure been given and processed?
(C15, S16)
(C16, S18)
(C17, S18)
(C18, S19)
(C19, S20)
Copyright, Lawrence M. Miller
*Chapters in the Team Kata book and Sections in the Video Course

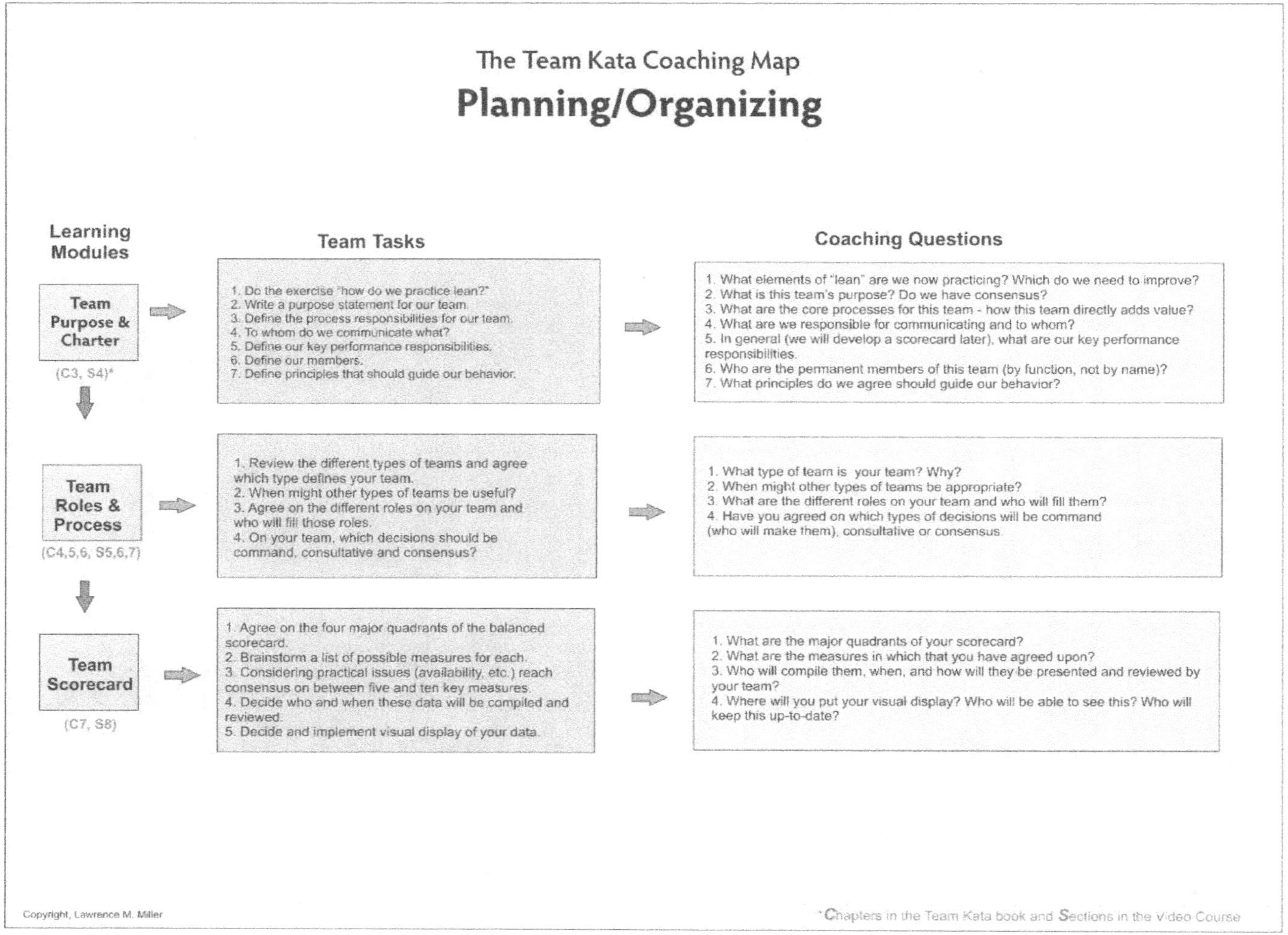

The Team Kata Coaching Map

Planning/Organizing

Learning Modules	Team Tasks	Coaching Questions
Team Purpose & Charter (C3, S4)*	1. Do the exercise "how do we practice lean?" 2. Write a purpose statement for our team. 3. Define the process responsibilities for our team. 4. To whom do we communicate what? 5. Define our key performance responsibilities. 6. Define our members. 7. Define principles that should guide our behavior.	1. What elements of "lean" are we now practicing? Which do we need to improve? 2. What is this team's purpose? Do we have consensus? 3. What are the core processes for this team - how this team directly adds value? 4. What are we responsible for communicating and to whom? 5. In general (we will develop a scorecard later), what are our key performance responsibilities. 6. Who are the permanent members of this team (by function, not by name)? 7. What principles do we agree should guide our behavior?
Team Roles & Process (C4,5,6, S5,6,7)	1. Review the different types of teams and agree which type defines your team. 2. When might other types of teams be useful? 3. Agree on the different roles on your team and who will fill those roles. 4. On your team, which decisions should be command, consultative and consensus?	1. What type of team is your team? Why? 2. When might other types of teams be appropriate? 3. What are the different roles on your team and who will fill them? 4. Have you agreed on which types of decisions will be command (who will make them), consultative or consensus.
Team Scorecard (C7, S8)	1. Agree on the four major quadrants of the balanced scorecard. 2. Brainstorm a list of possible measures for each. 3. Considering practical issues (availability, etc.) reach consensus on between five and ten key measures. 4. Decide who and when these data will be compiled and reviewed. 5. Decide and implement visual display of your data.	1. What are the major quadrants of your scorecard? 2. What are the measures in which that you have agreed upon? 3. Who will compile them, when, and how will they be presented and reviewed by your team? 4. Where will you put your visual display? Who will be able to see this? Who will keep this up-to-date?

*Chapters in the Team Kata book and Sections in the Video Course

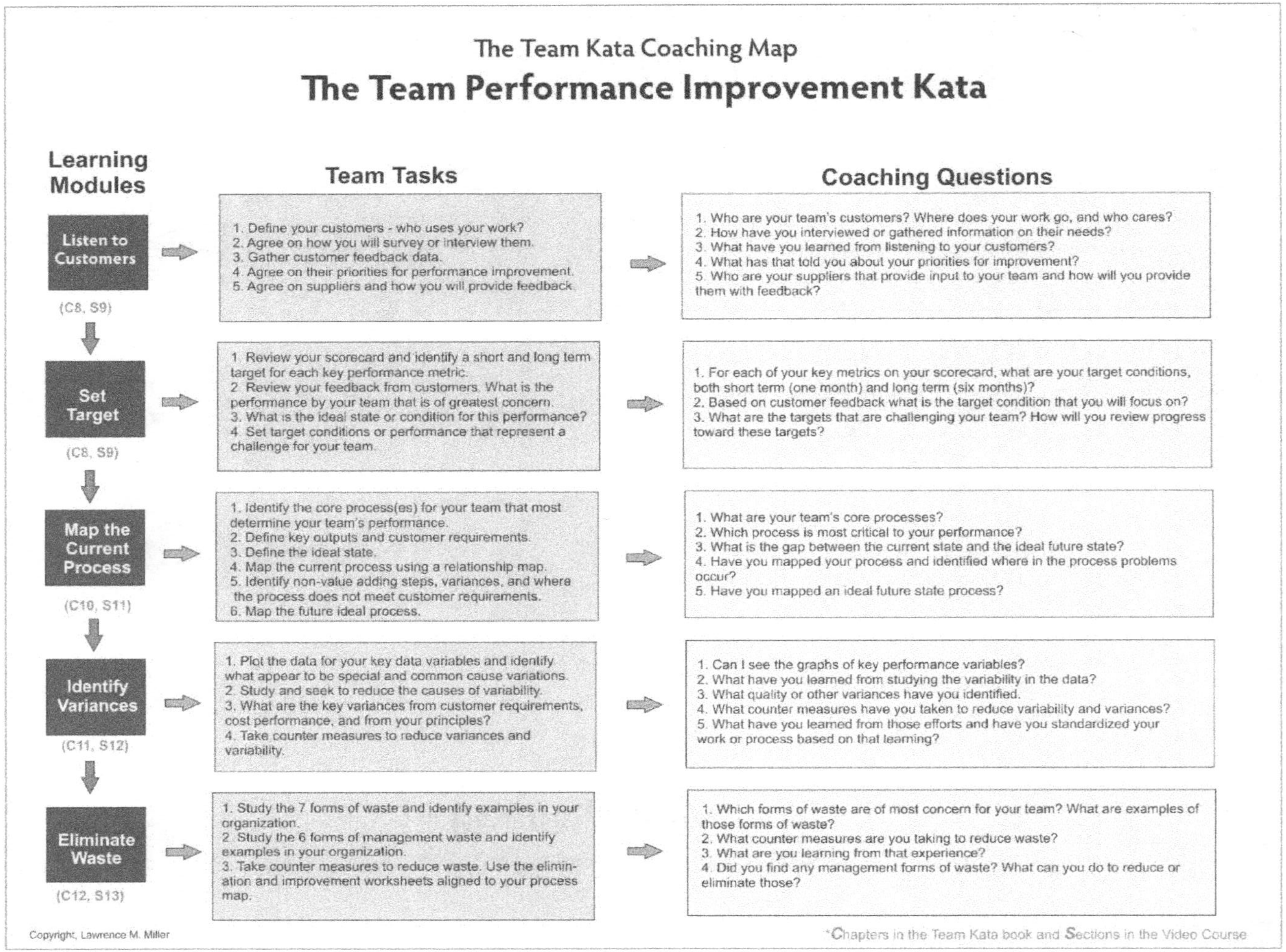

The Team Kata Coaching Map

The Team Performance Improvement Kata

Learning Modules	Team Tasks	Coaching Questions
Listen to Customers (C8, S9)	1. Define your customers - who uses your work? 2. Agree on how you will survey or interview them. 3. Gather customer feedback data. 4. Agree on their priorities for performance improvement. 5. Agree on suppliers and how you will provide feedback.	1. Who are your team's customers? Where does your work go, and who cares? 2. How have you interviewed or gathered information on their needs? 3. What have you learned from listening to your customers? 4. What has that told you about your priorities for improvement? 5. Who are your suppliers that provide input to your team and how will you provide them with feedback?
Set Target (C8, S9)	1. Review your scorecard and identify a short and long term target for each key performance metric. 2. Review your feedback from customers. What is the performance by your team that is of greatest concern. 3. What is the ideal state or condition for this performance? 4. Set target conditions or performance that represent a challenge for your team.	1. For each of your key metrics on your scorecard, what are your target conditions, both short term (one month) and long term (six months)? 2. Based on customer feedback what is the target condition that you will focus on? 3. What are the targets that are challenging your team? How will you review progress toward these targets?
Map the Current Process (C10, S11)	1. Identify the core process(es) for your team that most determine your team's performance. 2. Define key outputs and customer requirements. 3. Define the ideal state. 4. Map the current process using a relationship map. 5. Identify non-value adding steps, variances, and where the process does not meet customer requirements. 6. Map the future ideal process.	1. What are your team's core processes? 2. Which process is most critical to your performance? 3. What is the gap between the current state and the ideal future state? 4. Have you mapped your process and identified where in the process problems occur? 5. Have you mapped an ideal future state process?
Identify Variances (C11, S12)	1. Plot the data for your key data variables and identify what appear to be special and common cause variations. 2. Study and seek to reduce the causes of variability. 3. What are the key variances from customer requirements, cost performance, and from your principles? 4. Take counter measures to reduce variances and variability.	1. Can I see the graphs of key performance variables? 2. What have you learned from studying the variability in the data? 3. What quality or other variances have you identified. 4. What counter measures have you taken to reduce variability and variances? 5. What have you learned from those efforts and have you standardized your work or process based on that learning?
Eliminate Waste (C12, S13)	1. Study the 7 forms of waste and identify examples in your organization. 2. Study the 6 forms of management waste and identify examples in your organization. 3. Take counter measures to reduce waste. Use the elimination and improvement worksheets aligned to your process map.	1. Which forms of waste are of most concern for your team? What are examples of those forms of waste? 2. What counter measures are you taking to reduce waste? 3. What are you learning from that experience? 4. Did you find any management forms of waste? What can you do to reduce or eliminate those?

*Chapters in the Team Kata book and Sections in the Video Course

The Team Kata Coaching Map

The Team Performance Improvement Kata-2

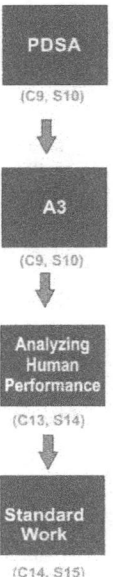

Learning Modules	Team Tasks	Coaching Questions
PDSA (C9, S10)	1. Identify key problems that will close the gap and move your scorecard. 2. Try the 5 Why's, root cause analysis. 3. Study and use the PDSA problem solving model on at least one problem. 4. What did you learn from each and when is each most appropriate?	1. What are the problems you are working on at this time? 2. Which problem solving model are you using? 3. What have you learned from that experience? 4. When you used the PDSA model, did you use the form and can I see what you did at each step?
A3 (C9, S10)	1. Decide to use the DIMPABA or traditional A3 model. 2. Take one more complex problem and go through the steps on the form. Implement counter measures or solutions. 3. With your team, discuss and agree when each model of problem solving is most appropriate. 4. Develop the habit of using a disciplined model of problem solving.	1.Which A3 model have you decided to use? 2. Have you identified a problem to solve using the A3? 3. Who is leading the A3 process and who is on the team going through that process. 4. Have you implemented counter measures to the problem? 5. What lessons have you learned from that experience?
Analyzing Human Performance (C13, S14)	1. Identify sources of the three forms of motivation. Purpose, Social and Situational, in your organization. 2. Identify at least one way to improve each. 3. Identify one behavior that you would like to improve and apply the ABC model to that behavior. 4. Apply the Performance Analysis model to one performance.	1. How do you feel your team can improve the sense of purpose among team members? How can you improve the power of social motivation? 2. What behavior did you seek to improve applying the ABC model? What did you learn from that experience? 3. Using the Performance Analysis model, what performance did you decide was a "Can't Do" versus "Won't Do?" Did you follow the rest of the model? 4. What are the major human performance challenges you face and how can you address those with the lessons in this section.
Standard Work (C14, S15)	1. For each of your team members, develop a standard work sheet. 2. Follow the process of reviewing standard work at each level. 3. Implement leader standard work. Be the example!	1. Ask to see the standard work sheets for each position. 2. When are these reviewed and by whom? Is this a positive learning experience? 3. How is standard work being updated and modified as learning occurs?

*Chapters in the Team Kata book and Sections in the Video Course

The Team Kata Coaching Map

Improve Effectiveness & Sustain

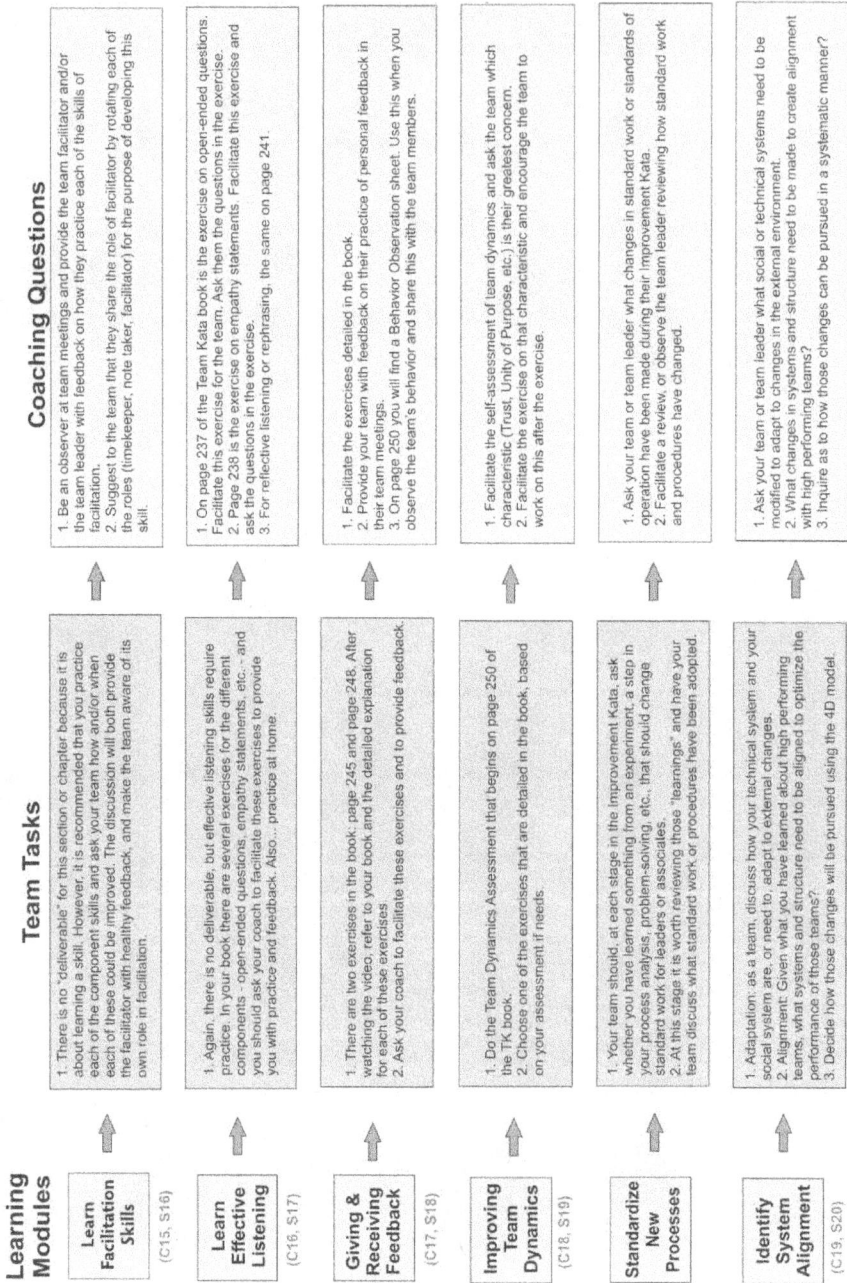

Learning Modules	Team Tasks	Coaching Questions
Learn Facilitation Skills (C15, S16)	1. There is no "deliverable" for this section or chapter because it is about learning a skill. However, it is recommended that you practice each of the component skills and ask your team how and/or when each of these could be improved. The discussion will both provide the facilitator with healthy feedback, and make the team aware of its own role in facilitation.	1. Be an observer at team meetings and provide the team facilitator and/or the team leader with feedback on how they practice each of the skills of facilitation. 2. Suggest to the team that they share the role of facilitator by rotating each of the roles (timekeeper, note taker, facilitator) for the purpose of developing this skill.
Learn Effective Listening (C16, S17)	1. Again, there is no deliverable, but effective listening skills require practice. In your book there are several exercises for the different components - open-ended questions, empathy statements, etc. - and you should ask your coach to facilitate these exercises to provide you with practice and feedback. Also… practice at home.	1. On page 237 of the Team Kata book is the exercise on open-ended questions. Facilitate this exercise for the team. Ask them the questions in the exercise. 2. Page 238 is the exercise on empathy statements. Facilitate this exercise and ask the questions in the exercise. 3. For reflective listening or rephrasing, the same on page 241.
Giving & Receiving Feedback (C17, S18)	1. There are two exercises in the book: page 245 and page 248. After watching the video, refer to your book and the detailed explanation for each of these exercises. 2. Ask your coach to facilitate these exercises and to provide feedback.	1. Facilitate the exercises detailed in the book. 2. Provide your team with feedback on their practice of personal feedback in their team meetings. 3. On page 250 you will find a Behavior Observation sheet. Use this when you observe the team's behavior and share this with the team members.
Improving Team Dynamics (C18, S19)	1. Do the Team Dynamics Assessment that begins on page 250 of the TK book. 2. Choose one of the exercises that are detailed in the book, based on your assessment if needs.	1. Facilitate the self-assessment of team dynamics and ask the team which characteristic (Trust, Unity of Purpose, etc.) is their greatest concern. 2. Facilitate the exercise on that characteristic and encourage the team to work on this after the exercise.
Standardize New Processes	1. Your team should, at each stage in the Improvement Kata, ask whether you have learned something from an experiment, a step in your process analysis, problem-solving, etc., that should change standard work for leaders or associates. 2. At this stage it is worth reviewing those "learnings" and have your team discuss what standard work or procedures have been adopted.	1. Ask your team or team leader what changes in standard work or standards of operation have been made during their Improvement Kata. 2. Facilitate a review, or observe the team leader reviewing how standard work and procedures have changed.
Identify System Alignment (C19, S20)	1. Adaptation: as a team, discuss how your technical system and your social system are, or need to, adapt to external changes. 2. Alignment: Given what you have learned about high performing teams, what systems and structure need to be aligned to optimize the performance of those teams? 3. Decide how those changes will be pursued using the 4D model.	1. Ask your team or team leader what social or technical systems need to be modified to adapt to changes in the external environment. 2. What changes in systems and structure need to be made to create alignment with high performing teams? 3. Inquire as to how those changes can be pursued in a systematic manner?

*Chapters in the Team Kata book and Sections in the Video Course

TEAM MEETING OBSERVATION AND EVALUATION

The following table is an observation checklist that you may use when sitting and observing a team meeting being conducted by the team's designated leader or facilitator. You can copy this checklist and use it to provide feedback to the team leader. It is one helpful way to structure a debriefing with your team leaders.

	Team Meeting Procedures:	**Notes:**
	The Agenda has been given to the team members before the meeting	
	Agenda includes critical components of an effective team meeting	
	• Data Review with Graphs	
	• Review of Previous Action Items	
	• Recognition for good performance	
	• One of more steps in problem-solving	
	The Leader was prepared for the meeting	
	Meeting starts on time with all members present	
	Meeting ends on time	

	No distracting interruptions during the meeting	
	Team follows their code of conduct	
	A copy of the team action record is distributed before the meeting	

1. **Performance Data Review:** **Notes:**

	Leaders has team performance data available	
	Data is visually presented on readable charts or graphs that are meaningful to the team	
	Team's public scorecard is up-to-date	
	Leader asks open ended questions about the data and how to improve performance	
	Leaders elicits agreement on performance problems and successes	
	Leader reinforces team members for good performance	
	Action plans are developed to improve performance	
	Action plans are in place that are improving performance	

2. Accountability: **Notes:**

	The leader or team members review each action item from previous meetings	
	Leader uses the "who, what and when" action planning format.	
	Leader asks someone to record action items and progress on action items.	
	The leader clarifies the decision style, when appropriate	

3. Facilitation Skills: **Notes:**

	Leader asks open-ended questions to gain participation	
	Leader encourages all to express their views by:	
	• Prompting the group to participate	
	• Prompting individuals to participate	
	• Reinforcing the group for participation	

	• Reinforcing individuals for their participation	
	Leader rephrases when appropriate	
	Leader expresses empathy when appropriate	
	Leader summarizes agreements, decisions, and action items	

4. Group Process Skills: **Notes:**

	Leaders keeps discussions focused on the topic	
	Leader controls the meeting in a positive manner	
	Leader ensures that all members support decisions	
	Leader encourages team members	

5. Problem-solving: **Notes:**

	Problems are identified using data analysis or brainstorming	
	Problems are clearly defined	
	Causes are analyzed using brainstorming	

	Causes are analyzed (80/20)	
	Solutions are generated through brainstorming	
	Solutions are evaluated	
	Consensus is reached on solutions	
	Action plans are agreed upon	
	Actions plans contain who, what, when	

6. Evaluation and Planning: **Notes:**

	The leader asks for a critique of the meeting	
	The leader acknowledges feedback and asks for alternative behavior and agreement is reached	
	Input for the next meeting is elicited	
	The leader thanks participants	

OBSERVATION FEEDBACK SUMMARY

Category	Positive Observations	Potential Improvements
1. Team Meeting Procedures		
2. Performance Data Review		
3. Accountability		
4. Facilitation Skills		
5. Group Process Skills		
6. Problem-solving		
7. Evaluation & Planning		

IMPROVING TEAM DYNAMICS

The purpose of this chapter is to develop relationships within the team that will allow open, honest, and trusting communications among team members.

TEAM DYNAMICS ASSESSMENT

Complete the following team dynamics assessment and have your coach compile the results and feed them back to the team.

TRUST:

1. I trust that when I offer my opinion to the group I will be heard and respected.

1__________2__________3__________4__________5
Not at all **Somewhat** **Very Much**

2. I trust that other members of the group are offering their honest opinions to the group.

1__________2__________3__________4__________5
Not at all **Somewhat** **Very Much**

3. I will not be "put-down" for offering an opinion that may be very different from others in the group.

1__________2__________3__________4__________5
Not at all **Somewhat** **Very Much**

4. Our discussion and opinions will stay inside this team and not be shared outside the team or used against another member.

1__________2__________3__________4__________5
Not at all **Somewhat** **Very Much**

HONEST STRAIGHT TALK:

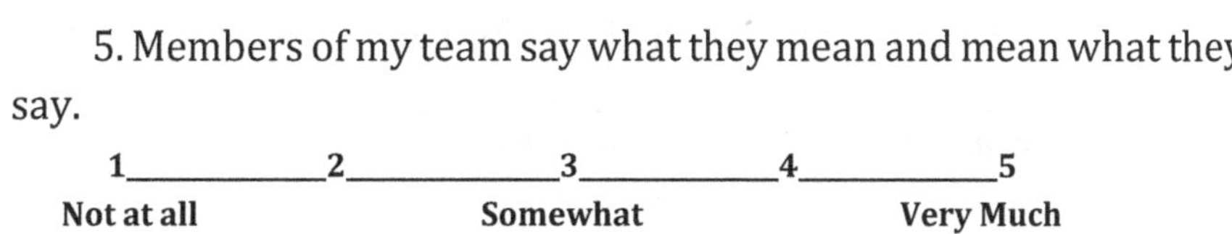

5. Members of my team say what they mean and mean what they say.

1__________2__________3__________4__________5
Not at all **Somewhat** **Very Much**

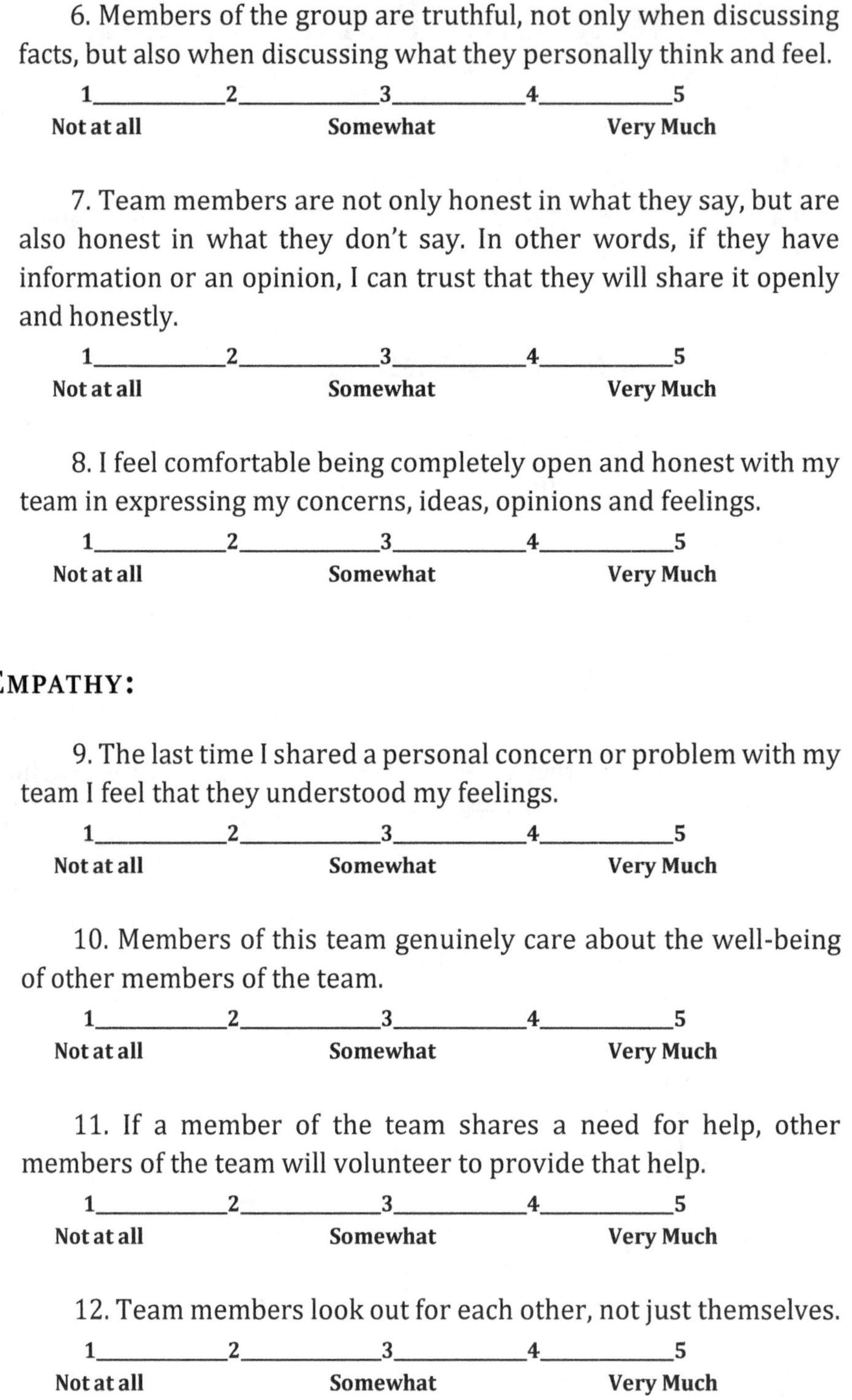

6. Members of the group are truthful, not only when discussing facts, but also when discussing what they personally think and feel.

1__________2__________3__________4__________5

Not at all **Somewhat** **Very Much**

7. Team members are not only honest in what they say, but are also honest in what they don't say. In other words, if they have information or an opinion, I can trust that they will share it openly and honestly.

1__________2__________3__________4__________5

Not at all **Somewhat** **Very Much**

8. I feel comfortable being completely open and honest with my team in expressing my concerns, ideas, opinions and feelings.

1__________2__________3__________4__________5

Not at all **Somewhat** **Very Much**

EMPATHY:

9. The last time I shared a personal concern or problem with my team I feel that they understood my feelings.

1__________2__________3__________4__________5

Not at all **Somewhat** **Very Much**

10. Members of this team genuinely care about the well-being of other members of the team.

1__________2__________3__________4__________5

Not at all **Somewhat** **Very Much**

11. If a member of the team shares a need for help, other members of the team will volunteer to provide that help.

1__________2__________3__________4__________5

Not at all **Somewhat** **Very Much**

12. Team members look out for each other, not just themselves.

1__________2__________3__________4__________5

Not at all **Somewhat** **Very Much**

UNITY OF PURPOSE:

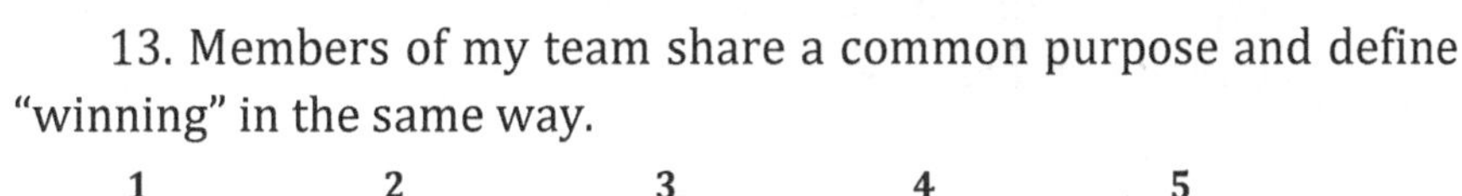

13. Members of my team share a common purpose and define "winning" in the same way.

1__________2__________3__________4__________5

Not at all **Somewhat** **Very Much**

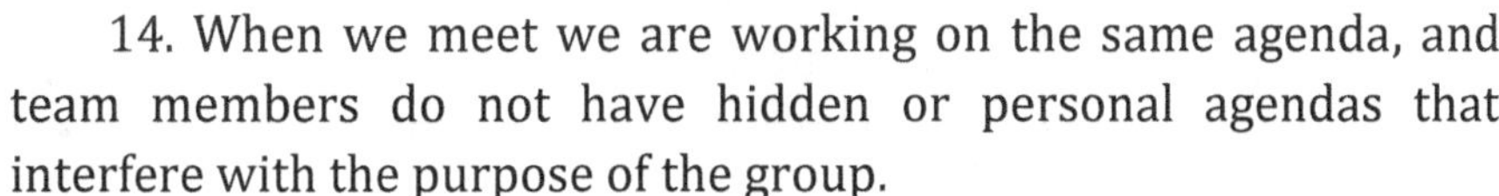

14. When we meet we are working on the same agenda, and team members do not have hidden or personal agendas that interfere with the purpose of the group.

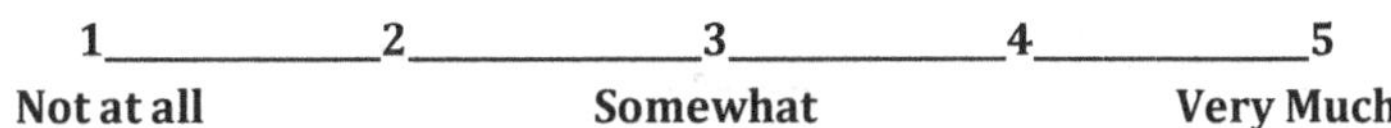

1__________2__________3__________4__________5

Not at all **Somewhat** **Very Much**

15. There is a high "sense of purpose" on the team, a desire to accomplish our mission.

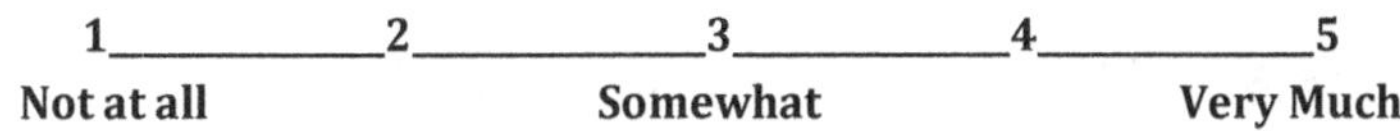

1__________2__________3__________4__________5

Not at all **Somewhat** **Very Much**

16. Our team feels united, as if we are working together as one cohesive unit.

1__________2__________3__________4__________5

Not at all **Somewhat** **Very Much**

APPRECIATION OF DIVERSITY:

17. In some ways I am different from other members of my team. Other team members recognize and appreciate these differences.

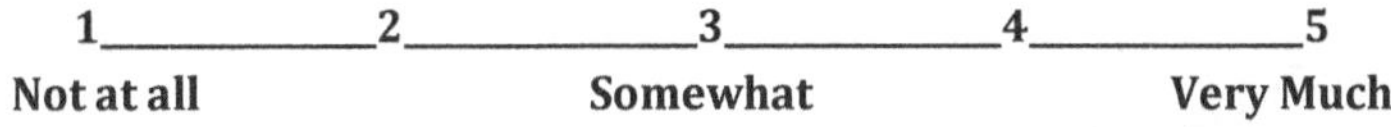

1__________2__________3__________4__________5

Not at all **Somewhat** **Very Much**

18. Members of the team speak in different "voices", some more assertive, some more quiet or reserved. All members are heard equally for the content of what they have to say, rather than how loudly they speak.

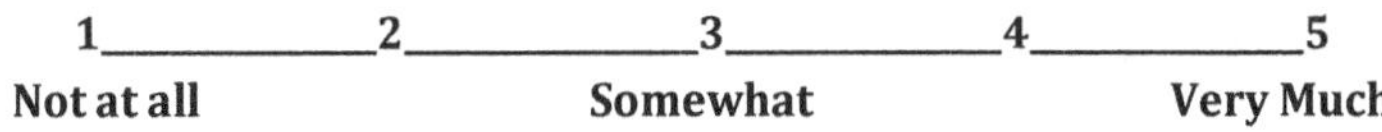

1__________2__________3__________4__________5

Not at all **Somewhat** **Very Much**

19. In every group there is a dominant culture. There are usually individuals who represent a sub-culture or minority

culture. Our team listens and respects the views of those representing these different cultures with respect and understanding.

1__________2__________3__________4__________5

Not at all **Somewhat** **Very Much**

20. Diversity of experience, perspectives and opinions is an asset to a team. It is the expression of this diversity that prevents "group-think." My team is diverse, and diverse views are expressed and well received by the team.

1__________2__________3__________4__________5

Not at all **Somewhat** **Very Much**

How Did Your Team Score?

Compile the average scores for each item and for each category. There is a potential score of twenty for each category.

Trust

1 2 3 4 5 6 7 8 9 10 11 12 13 14 15 16 17 18 19 20

Honest Straight Talk

1 2 3 4 5 6 7 8 9 10 11 12 13 14 15 16 17 18 19 20

Empathy

1 2 3 4 5 6 7 8 9 10 11 12 13 14 15 16 17 18 19 20

Unity of Purpose

1 2 3 4 5 6 7 8 9 10 11 12 13 14 15 16 17 18 19 20

Appreciation of Diversity

1 2 3 4 5 6 7 8 9 10 11 12 13 14 15 16 17 18 19 20

DEBRIEF:

In your team meeting, discuss the following questions and reach consensus on ways you can improve the inter-personal dynamics of your team. It is very important to keep in mind that EVERY team, every family, every community, every group of human beings, can improve how they deal with each other. The purpose is not to conclude that you are either good or bad. The purpose is to make continuous improvement in the human dynamics of your team.

When debriefing, agree on the rule "No one is to blame, or we are all to blame!"

1. Which category produced the highest score?

    a. Why do you believe you scored well in this category?

    b. What specific behavior contributed to this score?

____

____

____

2. Which category produced the lowest score?

    a. Why do you believe you scored low in this category?

    b. What specific behavior contributed to this low score?

____

____

____

____

3. Review the individual items and the scores for each item in the other categories.

   a. These scores suggest that we could improve what behavior to improve the inter-personal dynamics within our team?

____

____

____

____

Improving The Inter-Personal Dynamics of Your Team

Perhaps the first and most important thing any team can do to improve the dynamics within the team is to periodically "process" their own functioning as a team. Stop and think, reflect, and then discuss how your team is functioning. Doing this periodically, in an open and honest way is the most essential step in improving the inter-personal dynamics of any team.

Over the past years many exercises have been developed to improve the dynamics of teams. Some are done within the normal team setting, and others are experiential exercises that require going off-site for outdoor, more physical experiences.

One of the most effective exercises I have experienced was when a company leadership team decided to take on a service project as a team. This company was in a construction related business. They knew how to build things. They found that the local YWCA/YMCA needed to reconstruct the building that had been donated to them. Over a six month period this management team worked together to reconstruct the building. After doing this, the team reported that they learned more about each other, came to trust each other, and had better feelings toward each other than ever before. This was a true "action-learning" experience that both improved the performance and "spirit" of the team, and also improved the company's relations in the community.

Behavior Observations

Use the following to record observations of behavior in preparation for giving feedback to another individual. Remember to pinpoint behavior in a way that two persons will see the same thing. Do not record "attitudes" or your own feelings.

Helpful Behaviors	Effects on You and the Team	Possible Alternatives
Unhelpful Behaviors	**Effects on You and the Team**	**Possible Alternatives**

Trust Building Exercises

1. Two Truths and a Lie

This is an easy and effective first exercise. It is an "ice-breaker" and a simple get-to-know each other game. The purpose of the game is to learn something about each team member that you would not learn through the routine of team meetings focused on work.

Directions: Ask each member of the team to write down three things. Two of them are true things that other members of the group are not likely to know. The third one is a lie.

Then go around the room and have each person read their three things. Ask everyone to guess which one is the lie. After everyone guesses, then ask the person to share which are true and which was a lie.

Debrief: Make it simple. Ask the group what was the most surprising thing they learned about a team member.

2. If I Made a Movie...

This exercise is somewhat similar to the above, but it gets to a more serious level of knowing other members of the group. To share hopes, dreams and fears requires trust in other members. This is another practice session in building trust.

Facilitator: It is important that group members share their stories voluntarily. Some may not be comfortable sharing and they should be invited, but not pressured to share.

Directions: If I made a movie and it was about my life, what scene would be a defining moment in the movie? It can be tragic or heroic. Describe the scene and why it would be a defining moment of my life. This can be an actual scene or one that you make up to illustrate a key event or transition in your life. If you were casting an actor to play you in this movie, who would you cast in your role?

Ask each member of the group to spend ten to fifteen minutes defining the scene and which actor would play them in the movie.

Then, ask members to volunteer to share their scene and the actor. Ask them what this scene tells us that is important about their life.

Debrief: After each person has shared their story, ask the group "What have we learned about another team member that helps us understand them better?"

3. The Mine Field

This is a very flexible exercise. It can be done inside or outside (more fun outside). The purpose is to learn to trust a partner and follow their guidance.

Things you will need: 1) an area to make a large circle in which you will distribute the "mines"; 2) blindfolds; 3) objects to use as "mines."

Directions: Select an area, a room with a good bit of floor space, or outside. Identify some objects that you can use as "mines." These will be things that the participants will have to navigate around and avoid bumping in to. These should be objects that will not break if knocked over, such as rubber cones or a stack of coffee cups.

Create a large circle with the "mines," 15-20 of them, randomly arranged within the circle.

The facilitator should establish a calm and serious tone for the exercise which helps develop trust in the group.

- Form the group into pairs of two. One of the pair will be blindfolded and will follow instructions of the other. This can be done twice so each person plays each role.

- The blindfolded persons may not talk during the exercise. The facilitators will take them by the hand and move them to a randomly selected point on the circle. Then the facilitator will instruct them how to walk to the opposite side of the circle without walking on a mine. Only one participant is in the circle at a time.

- Allow the participants five minutes to plan their verbal commands and how instructions will be given.

- Count the number of times each participants hit a mine. The team with the fewest hits wins the game. You can do the exercise several times to allow the participants to develop skill at the task and at giving and receiving instructions.

- You can also try the exercise with all pairs working at the same time, in other words all the blindfolded participants will be going through the circle at the same time. The trick will be to get to the other side and not bump into either the mines or the other participants. This will also require some cooperative behavior between pairs.

This exercise can be made very easy or very hard by increasing or decreasing the number of mines or by doing it with only one or more than one person in the circle at any one time. The facilitator needs to make a judgment as to how comfortable the participants are and how much of a challenge is appropriate for their level of trust.

The facilitator should be prepared to call "time-out" if he or she perceives that a blindfolded person is panicking or becoming overly frustrated. It is best that this exercise be done after one of the previous exercises, rather than as a first exercise.

The facilitator should be aware that some adults have had actual experiences with mine fields and this exercise could cause a stress reaction. Ask the group if anyone has such an experience. If so, rename it "The Obstacle Course." (Why not just CALL it the obstacle course to start with?)

Debrief: After the exercise is over, discuss the following questions:

- On a scale of 1-10, how much did you trust your partner to get you through the minefield at the beginning.

- By the time the exercise was over, how much did you trust that partner? What does this tell us about developing trust?

- What behavior led to increased trust, or reduced trust?

- What does this tell us about developing trust in the workplace?

- What communication strategies worked best?
- What did I learn about myself and how I react to stress?

STRAIGHT TALK EXERCISES

Trust and honesty are two sides of the same coin. The more honest we are, the more we will be trusted by others. The kind of honesty that we are concerned with on the team is not honesty about telling lies. It is more about "straight-talk," the honesty that is sharing what you really feel, saying what is on your mind. Group cohesion and group decision-making are often hindered by members of the group simply not "honestly" sharing what they think and feel. This type of honesty may also be called "being open" or willing to share what is inside of you.

6. THE TRUTHS I DENY MYSELF

One of the ways that we are not entirely honest is not being honest with ourselves. We all (at least most of us) tell ourselves little falsehoods to avoid confronting something we may want to avoid confronting. The purpose of this exercise is to initiate openness and sharing among team members.

Directions: Ask each team member to write down two different ways that "I fool myself" or "I am not completely honest with myself." It is important that the facilitator model, give examples, him or herself. So start by sharing two things you, the facilitator, do to fool yourself. For example:

- I tell myself I am trying to lose weight and then I sneak ice cream with maple syrup on top, late at night before I go to bed.
- I am trying to save money by spending less, yet I cannot resist buying some latest gadget because it is the newest, best whatever, even though I know I don't really need it.

Give the group five or ten minutes to write down their little falsehoods that they tell themselves. Then ask the members of the group to share. It is best not to go around the room, but just ask for volunteers so members who are uncomfortable don't feel pressured.

When others are sharing, no one else should make any disapproving comment ("Oh my God! I can't believe you do that!") Remember that the purpose of this exercise is to confront the common habit of denial within all of us.

Debrief: The facilitator should point out that we all have things in common. What are the common habits that we shared?

Ask the group, what does this tendency to not confront things, even to ourselves, tell us about how we communicate or work together?

Do we fail to be open and honest with others for the same reasons we may fail to be honest with ourselves?

UNITY OF PURPOSE

Teams are most successful when the members of the team share common goals and common purpose. Your team developed a charter that included a purpose statement, and this should be your shared purpose. But we all have our own purpose, our own goals or concerns, and sometimes these personal issues are more dominant than our collective purpose.

7. THE PURPOSE DIAGRAM

This exercise is intended to elicit personal reflection on the part of team members and develop understanding of the goals we have in common.

Directions: This exercise has three parts: first, private reflection; second, developing an "affinity diagram"; third, debrief. This exercise can be used as practice in developing an affinity diagram, a skill that will be useful in other activities.

- Explain to the group that we will use an "affinity diagram" to share our understanding of our own purpose and goals and how they are common or different.
- Explain what an affinity diagram is: *A brainstorming and decision technique designed to generate and then sort a large number of ideas into related groups in a visual display.* Ask the group to follow the following steps to generate this diagram.

Step 1: Describe the Problem or Issue: The issue in this case is "why are we here?" What is our goal or purpose that brings us together as a team? What do I hope to gain, achieve or experience by participating on this team?

Step 2: Generate ideas: Distribute small pads of post-it-notes to each member of the team. Ask them to write down, each on a separate note, as many ideas that answer the question as they can think of. The ideas can be big ones or small ones. Give the group ten minutes to think about and write down their ideas.

Step 3: Display the ideas. Post the ideas on a wall, or a table in a *random* manner. Just get them up so they can all be seen. Then ask them to start studying all of the ideas that have been posted. IMPORTANT: ask them to do this and the next step in SILENCE. This is hard for most teams. Explain that this may be a new experience, but we will learn that sometimes the team can learn and decide without talking at all.

Step 4: Sort the ideas into related groups. Ask the team members physically sort the cards into groupings, **without talking**, using the following process:

- Start by looking for two ideas that seem related in some way. Place them together in a column off to one side.
- Look for ideas that are related to those you've already set aside and add them to that group.
- Look for other ideas that are related to each other and establish new groups. This process is repeated until the team has placed all of the ideas in groups.

NOTE: Ideally, all of the ideas can be sorted into related groups. If there are some "loners" that don't fit any of the groups, don't force them into groupings where they don't belong. Let them stand alone under their own headers or under a "miscellaneous" heading.

Step 5: Create header cards for the groups. A header is an idea that captures the essential link among the ideas contained in a group of cards. This idea is written on a single card or post-it-note and must consist of a phrase or sentence that clearly conveys the meaning, even to people who are not on the team. The team develops headers for the groups by...

- o Finding already existing cards within the groups that will serve well as headers and placing them at the top of the group of related cards.

- o Alternatively, discussing and agreeing on the wording of cards created specifically to be headers.
- o Once you have completed the affinity diagram ask the group to discuss what they learned from doing this. Ask the following questions:

- o What does this tell us about the goals and purpose that we share?
- o What does this tell us about how we are different in our goals and purpose?
- o Does this tell us anything about how we function as a team, or how we should function as a team?
- o Summarize by pointing out the importance of common purpose and how this is present or how it needs to be developed by the team.

APPRECIATION OF DIVERSITY:

The subject of diversity in the workplace is one that has been addressed by many forms of training. Most of this has focused on two issues: race and gender. Over the past fifty years our workplace has changed dramatically in the increased number of women and African-Americans, Hispanics and Asians in the workplace. There are many specialized workshops to address how we respond to these changes.

You may think of the following exercise as merely an introduction to this subject, and an opportunity to recognize, understand and appreciate all of the different forms of diversity that are present on our team.

8. WE ARE ALL DIFFERENT – WE ARE ALL THE SAME

Among the members of any team there are similarities and differences that affect the way we view problems and solutions. These differences also affect our manner of speech, our emotions, and how we interpret events. The purpose of this exercise is to share some of those differences among team members and how they influence our behavior.

Directions: Explain that the purpose of this exercise is to recognize some of the differences -- the unique qualities and experience -- of each member of our team.

- Ask the team members to spend ten to fifteen minutes alone, reflecting on how they may be different from all or the majority of other team members. These differences may be ethnic, age, gender, religion, work experience, education, personality or other life experience. Ask them to write down three ways that they are unique or different.
- The facilitator will then ask that each member share his or her three differences.
- The facilitator will instruct all the team members to listen well and think about how the differences being described present the team with an asset, some value or virtue that can be appreciated and contribute to the team.
- Immediately after an individual shares his or her differences, the facilitator will ask the group "How do you feel those qualities or experiences can be an asset to our team?" Let the group share their thoughts for a few moments and then go on to the next person.

Debrief: After everyone has shared and received this appreciation from the group, ask the team to spend three minutes just thinking about and reflecting on what they heard. Then ask the group the following questions:

- o How did the group's response to your diversity cause you to feel?
- o How did it make you feel about the team in general?
- o How may what you learned affect the future behavior of the team?

9. Team Commitment

The purpose of this exercise is to help the team explore the meaning of "commitment" to the team and each other and to practice giving and receiving feedback on their commitment.

There are four stages of this exercise: first, brainstorming indicators of commitment; second, private assessment of each individual's demonstration of those indicators; third, sharing and processing that feedback; and fourth, reflection and sharing commitments to future behavior. The exercise is structured to provide confidential feedback and minimize the possibility of painful confrontations that sometimes occur over this issue.

You will need a large number of post-it-notes, preferably of the same color so as not to indicate which member is providing which feedback.

Directions:

1. **Identifying Indicators:** Brainstorm what "commitment" means in a team setting. Ask the group, "How do you know it when you see it?" Or, "What pinpointed behaviors demonstrate that a member is committed to the success of the team?" Also, ask "What behavior indicates personal commitment to each other?"

- Generate a list of as many ideas as come to mind within ten minutes. This will probably be ten to twenty indicators such as "attends meetings regularly;" "participates in problem-solving and discussion;" or, "follows through on action items."
- Combine similar indicators. Your goal is to get down to only five indicators. Be sure that they are still pinpointed, observable behavior.
- Vote on the five that are most important and most reliable indicators of commitment to the team.

2. **Assessing Fellow Team Members:** On the following page is a sheet to record each person's evaluation of the other members of the team.

- Place the five indicators across the five columns titled "Indicators of Commitment." Each member should have a sheet like that on the following page. This sheet should be kept private by that member.
- Place the names of the other team members down the left hand column.
- Ask each member to rate each other member on each of these qualities using a ten-point scale. You can give the team fifteen minutes to do this in the meeting, or (and this is preferable) give them time between meetings to think about their assessment and complete the ratings during the time between this and the next meeting.

3. **Sharing Feedback:** The purpose of the following is to allow for each team member to receive absolutely frank and honest feedback without public discussion that could be painful or humiliating. The facilitator should keep in mind that it is often difficult for members to give public feedback and this leads to individuals receiving little or no feedback on their behavior.

- On a wall, the facilitator should make a table, somewhat like that on the following page, with the team member's names to the left in a column, and column headings for each of the indicators.

- Pass out post-it-notes to the team members. Ask them to write their ratings on the adhesive side of the post-it-note. It will help if they write the indicator on the visible side, such as "Attendance." This way, when they are placed on the wall, the side with the indicator will be visible and the rating will not be visible.

- For each other team member, each participant will write their rating on five notes, one for each indicator. They will then place them on the wall in the appropriate column and row.

- When all the notes have been placed on the wall, ask each individual to gather up their notes, keeping track of which indicator they represent. Returning to their seat, they should then average their scores for each item.

4. **Reflection and Commitment:** Give the team fifteen or twenty minutes to read and average their scores. Ask them to consider sharing the following based on the feedback they have received:

- What is one thing you will do in the future to strengthen your commitment to the success of the team?

- What help would you like to receive from other team members in the future?

Team Commitment Assessment					
Team Member	Indicators of Commitment				
Score each team member on each indicator on a 1 to 10 scale. 1 would indicate that the team member never demonstrates this behavior; 5 that they demonstrate this sometimes; and 10 that they demonstrate this to a very high degree.					

How far Along the Lean Journey Are We?

Which of the following have you implemented and How would you describe that implementation?

Lean Practices	Not at all	Just begun	Partially Implemented	Mostly Implemented	Fully Implemented	Future Action Plans
1. We have done Value Stream Mapping of our processes						
2. We have studied and eliminated waste						
3. Process Maps are visible to those at the Gemba						
4. We are eliminating quality variances from our process						

5. PDCA and/or A3 problem solving is visible in the work area						
6. We have reduced change over cycle time (SMED)						
7. Employees are empowered to stop the line or operation when they see a problem						
8. We measure and are reducing work in process inventory						
9. We have implemented and maintained 5S						
10. We have created a self-directed team process among the workforce						
11. Management teams are trained and are practicing the same skills.						
12. We implementing problem-solving or kaizen teams						

13. We have a process for encouraging individual suggestions						
14. We have designed jobs for cross-training to increase job flexibility						
15. We have instituted a system of rewards for improved performance						
16. Our managers practice 4 to 1						
17. We have a process for work standardization						
18. We have implemented Leader Standard Work						
19. We have empowered employees to make improvements to their work process						

20. Managers have aligned their own behavior and practices to the principles of Lean						
21. We celebrate improvements in both process and performance						
22. There is visual display (graphs) of team performance in the work area						
23. We design and align our sub-systems to strategy employing "catch ball" or Interactive planning.						

GLOSSARY

- 5S: The 5S's are Sort, Set in order, Shine, Standardize, and Sustain. 5S is a common tool and component of a lean workplace. The Five S program focuses on having visual order, organization, cleanliness and standardization. The results you can expect from a Five S program are: improved profitability, efficiency, service and safety.
- 5 Why's: The 5 Why's is a simple problem-solving technique that helps you to get to the root cause of a problem quickly. Made popular in the 1970s by the Toyota Production System, the 5 Whys strategy involves looking at any problem and asking: "Why?" and "What caused this problem?"
- 7 Forms of Waste: Waste is the use of any material or resource beyond what the customer requires and is willing to pay for. Shigeo Shingo identified "Seven" forms of waste (Plus one – The eighth waste, under-utilization of people) These 7 forms of waste are 1) Over production, 2) Inventory, 3) Motion, 4) Waiting, 5) Transportation, 6) Over-processing, 7) Scrap or rework.
- A3: An A3 is literally a size of paper (297 × 420 mm). However, it has become popular in lean management as a simple and structured form of problem-solving that can fit on or be displayed on one A3 sized paper.
- A4: An A4 is a size of paper. However, it has become known for an even simpler problem-solving process than an A3. It is a one sheet PDCA cycle problem-solving tool. (see PDCA)
- ABC Model: Stands for Antecedents, Behavior and Consequences. This is a model for changing behavior, whether at work or in any setting. Doing an ABC analysis is a way of analyzing why someone may be behaving in a given way and what can be done to change that behavior.
- Action Planning: After deciding on a solution to a problem, a team should develop an action plan that clearly states what steps are going to be taken to implement a solution; who is going to do them; and, when are they going to be done. Action plans are generally reviewed at each team meeting.

- Affinity Diagram: An affinity diagram is a component of brainstorming in which participants write ideas down on Post-it-Notes, then put them on a wall, and then silently organize them into like blocks of notes.
- Antecedents: A stimulus that precedes a behavior and acts as a stimulus or cue for that behavior to occur.
- Balanced Scorecard: A team or management scorecard that includes four types of measures: Financial, learning and development, customer satisfaction and process measures. This concept was developed and promoted in a book by Kaplan and Norton.
- Behavior Analysis: The application of behavioral psychology to behavior in a natural setting. Also referred to as *behavior management* or *performance management*.
- Behavior Management: A term used to describe the application of behavior analysis or behavior modification in the work place. It generally involves seeking to employ positive reinforcement to increase the strength and learning of desired behavior.
- Behavioral psychology: That school of psychology developed by B.F. Skinner and others that states that behavior is learned a function of the contingencies of reinforcement in the environment. Behavioral psychology is based on the experimental analysis of behavior in which antecedent stimuli and consequences to behavior are controlled and modified, and the resulting changes in rate of behavior are monitored.
- Brainstorming: This is one component of both problem-solving and group decision-making. It is a way to bring out the creativity of the group by focusing on generating ideas while not judging them. There are many methods of brainstorming but they all include the element of suspending judgment, allowing, even encouraging, wild and crazy ideas so that each idea may stimulate another.
- Cause-and-Effect Diagram: A cause and effect diagram is also known as a fishbone diagram because it looks something like the skeleton of a fish. At the backbone of the diagram is the definition of a problem. Then each of the major parts of the skeleton are labeled (and this is only one way of many) People, Process, Materials, Equipment, Information. Then you use this to brainstorm possible causes under each of these categories.
- Continuous Improvement: Continuous improvement is one of the fundamental ideas of lean management. It is based on the simple idea

that every process can always be improved in some increment. It is a process in which all employees engaged in the work are encouraged to participate in thinking about better ways to do things, conducting experiments, and agreeing on improved standard work.

- Cycle Time: A cycle time is the time from the beginning to the end of a work process. There are generally two types of cycle time: CT = The actual Cycle Time from beginning to end, and VCT=Value Adding Cycle Time. In other words, if you look at your daily work process, that may be eight hours, how much of that time is actually adding value to your customers? It is usually a fraction of the actual time. In lean terms, the remaining time is considered "waste."
- Empathy: Empathy is the capacity to recognize and, to some extent, share feelings (such as sadness or happiness) that are being experienced by another. Empathy is one of the effective listening skills that enables another person to express their thoughts and feelings.
- Facilitation: Facilitation is the skill or art of helping others participate in group problem-solving or decision-making. There are a set of skills that are components of effective facilitation and these include clarifying topics, active listening, conflict resolution, and helping a group reach and clarify a decision.
- Feedback: Feedback is information on performance that is "fed back" to the group or individual in control of that performance. Feedback is not necessarily positive or negative, but may simply be information on performance. Feedback is the most essential element of all systems of human performance.
- Fishbone Diagrams: See cause and effect diagrams.
- Four to One: The practice of recognizing four desirable behaviors to every one negative. Based on the research of Dr. Ogden Lindsley who found that the optimum rate of positive to negative in classrooms was 3.57 to 1.
- Gemba: Gemba is a Japanese word meaning "the real place where work gets done." It refers to the place where value is created in a work system. Being "on-the-spot" is another term meaning being where the work gets done. This is an important concept in lean management and it expresses the value of managers "going and seeing" what is really happening where the work is being done.

- Gemba Walk: The Gemba walk is simply that act of managers talking a walk around the work place and observing, learning, from those doing the work. In manufacturing it is recommended that plant managers take frequent Gemba walks to be in touch with the real work.
- Kaizen: Kaizen is the Japanese word for continuous improvement. It is one of the core philosophies and practices of lean management. Kaizen is intended to be practiced by all employees, at every level, engaged in every work process in the organization.
- Kaizen Event: A kaizen event is an intensified and short effort to make a major improvement in a process. It generally involves a cross-functional team of employees who work for a period, such as a week, studying a process to solve a problem and make a recommendation at the end of that period.
- Kata: A discipline of practice that develops a habit.
- Leader Standard Work: Leader standard work (LSW) is a process by which standard work, activities that are to be done daily, weekly or monthly, are defined by or for a manager. LSW involves the regular review of the completion and lessons learned from these activities by the manager at the next level above.
- Lean Management: Lean management is the set of management and work practices derived from the Toyota Production System (TPS). These include the elimination of waste, continuous improvement, and involvement of all employees in improvement activities. Lean and TPS are not a static set of practices, but are continually evolving as lessons are learned from application in different settings such as health care.
- Lean Process: A lean process is one in which every step adds value, speed through the process is optimized, there are no interruptions or re-work, and those who work in the process seek continuous improvement.
- Continuous Improvement: Continuous improvement is the merger of the lessons from lean management and those learned from the implementation of self-directed teams and the socio-technical system (STS) design of high performance work systems.
- PDCA Cycle: The PDCA (Plan, Do, Check and Act) cycle of problem-solving is also known as the Schewhart Cycle after Walter Schewhart a pioneer in the quality field. During the quality movement it was adopted

as a common problem-solving model at many companies. The PDCA cycle is best used for relatively simple problems, although you can place many different methods or steps within these four major steps.

- PDSA: This is essentially the same as the PDCA cycle of problem-solving: Plan, Do, Study, Act. This is the term used at ThedaCare and is more popular in healthcare organizations.
- Performance Analysis: A model of problem-solving human behavior. It is based on the work of Robert Mager and Peter Pipe who suggested that we ask "Is the problem a *can't do*, or a *won't do* problem?" In other words, does the individual have the required skill or knowledge, or is it a motivation problem.
- Performance Management: This term has two different usages. One is another term to describe behavior management or applied behavior analysis in the work setting. A second describes the process of individual performance appraisal and the development of periodic personal improvement plans, generally negotiated between an employee and his or her manager.
- Positive Reinforcement: In behavioral psychology or applied behavior analysis positive reinforcement is the presentation of a stimulus following a behavior that results in a subsequent increase in the rate of that behavior.
- Process: A process is a set of related activities that together produce a desired outcome. All processes have both input and output. The process transforms input to a value adding output. Teams are generally organized around, and take responsibility for, a defined process.
- Process Management Teams: A team that owns and takes responsibility for the continuous improvement of a defined process.
- Process Maps: A visual display of a process that illustrates each step in a process and their chronological relationship to one another. It describes the flow of the process. Process mapping allows a team to define cycle times, identify waste and variances in the process.
- Process Measures: Measures of process performance. These measures may be derived from within the process or at the end of a process. For example, if you are cooking a turkey dinner (a process) you may take a measure of the temperature of the meat while it is cooking (a measure

within the process), and you may measure the satisfaction of the guests when they are finished eating the turkey (end of process measure).

- Reflective Listening: Also known as rephrasing or active listening. Reflective listening is somewhat like holding up a mirror, a reflection, of what you think another person meant to say. For example, "In other words I hear you saying that you enjoy doing that job." This gives the other person the opportunity to say "Well, no, that isn't really what I meant." Or, "Yes, that's right." The other person may clarify and will feel that he or she has genuinely been heard.
- Scorecards: A score card is an agreed upon set of metrics that reflect the performance of a team. See "balanced scorecard." Scorecards are best visually displayed and reviewed regularly.
- Self-Directed Teams: Also known as autonomous or semi-autonomous teams, self-directed teams take responsibility for managing a process and continuously improving that process. While no team is ultimately "self-managed", the process of self-directed teams seeks to maximize the responsibility and maturity of a team to manage performance. Continuous Improvement is a self-directed team process.
- Shaping Behavior: Shaping is a concept of behavior analysis. Shaping is the successive reinforcement of approximations to a terminal goal set of responses or skill. In other words, when your child is first learning to play the piano, you praise (reinforce) small improvements and effort, rather than waiting for the ultimate performance.
- Six Sigma: An improvement process first developed at Motorola and an extension of the total quality movement. It relies heavily on statistical methods and has been used predominantly in manufacturing. A six sigma process is one in which 99.99966% of the products manufactured are statistically expected to be free of defects (3.4 defects per million).
- Socio-Technical Systems (STS): A process developed, originally at the Tavistock Institute in Great Britain by Fred Emery and Eric Trist to improve both the productivity of the work system while at the same time improving the social system. The theory of STS is that there is one whole-system, comprised of both social and technical components that are interdependent. Failing to change one element sub-optimizes any change effort.
- Special Cause: Dr. W. Edwards Deming described the statistical evidence of a process *in control* in which all of the causes of variation are within

three standard deviations of the mean. The cause of variation is common to the system and can only be improved by changing the system itself.

- Standard Work: A set of activities that have been agreed to be the best way to perform any work activity. Standard work is the best way we know now to perform a work process. However, continuous improvement will find better ways that will then become standard work.
- Statistical Variation: A set of statistical recording of performance that define a mean of that set and the variations around that mean.
- Team Charter: A document that defines a team's purpose, its processes, its customers and the principles by which it will function.
- TQM: Total Quality Management, a set of practices that involves a focus on the requirements of customers (or customers), the use of statistical measures of quality performance, teams improving quality and customer service at every level of the organization.
- Value Stream Mapping: Mapping the work flow, or processes, in a manner that identifies the points where value is added and non-value adding activities, or waste.
- Variances or Variation: A variance may be described statistically, or it may simply be something that deviates or varies from how things should be done in order to meet customer requirements. A variance is a problem.
- Waste: Any activity that does not directly add value to the product or service delivered to a customer.
- Whole-System Architecture: Another term used for socio-technical systems design in which all elements of an organization's systems are examined together to assess how they enhance or reduce the quality of product or service to customers.

INDEX

www.ingramcontent.com/pod-product-compliance
Lightning Source LLC
Chambersburg PA
CBHW061419210326
41598CB00035B/6265
* 9 7 8 0 9 8 9 3 2 3 2 9 1 *